A CPAS HA

YOUNG PEOPLE AND THE BIBLE

Phil Moon

Marshall Pickering
An Imprint of HarperCollins*Publishers*

Marshall Pickering is an Imprint of
HarperCollins*Religious*,
Part of HarperCollins*Publishers*,
77–85 Fulham Palace Road, London W6 8JB

First published in Great Britain
in 1992 by Marshall Pickering

1 3 5 7 9 10 8 6 4 2

A catalogue record for this book is
available from the British Library

ISBN 0 551 02371-6

Printed and bound in Great Britain by
HarperCollinsManufacturing Glasgow

For Anna

Acknowledgements

This book isn't a one-man show. I have been helped immensely by a large number of people. Thanks to those who have helped and moulded my thinking. Thanks to those who read early drafts and made penetrating comments. They've all been taken on board, but sometimes I disagreed! Andrew Moore's sensitive and astute theological insights, Ken Moulder's razor-sharp brain, Al and Jo Horn's attention to detail, Clive Grinham's gentle assertiveness, and Graham and Julie Burrows' down to earth practicalities immediately spring to mind, but there were many others too.

Thank you to those who typed it. Marjorie Seaman, Heather Linnecar, Kate Hunt and Miriam Dow all did an outstanding job.

Most of all, my thanks go to British Rail, whose erratic service from Paddington to Leamington Spa gave me plenty of time for thinking, reading, praying . . . and writing.

All the key examples come from resources which either have already been published by CPAS or will be published within the next year or so. They are the copyright of CPAS and are used here by the Society's kind permission. The ones already published are:

> *Growing More Like Jesus* (used in chapter 2)
> *Mark, Now Teach the Gospel* (used in chapter 3)
> *All Together Forever* (used in chapter 5)

Contents

1

The Best Job in the World – The Role of Today's Youth Leader

Teaching the Bible is the distinctive job of the Christian youth leader. We neglect it at our peril.

Yet we seldom think of a youth leader as a Bible teacher. Surely we're friends, counsellors, a shoulder to cry on. We're entertainers, people who get on well with teenagers. We're people they respect, we're surrogate mums and dads, we're social workers . . .

Yes, you will probably need to be a bit of all of these in your work as a leader.

But the one thing you cannot afford *not* to be, is a Bible teacher. That is also the one thing your young people cannot afford you *not* to be either.

The Bible is no ordinary book. When we read the Bible we are being dealt with by God, and that is not always a comfortable experience. The Bible criticises us, chastises us, and wants to change and reshape us. The Bible is God speaking, and its supreme purpose is to instruct its readers for salvation. How therefore can we possibly ignore it? How can we not teach it to our groups?

> All scripture is inspired by God and profitable for teaching, reproof, correction and for training in righteousness that the man of God may be thoroughly equipped for every good work (2 Timothy 3:16).
> When we open the Bible and begin to read it we are exposing ourselves to the voice of God who made us and who speaks to us with authority. (C Wright, *User's Guide to the Bible*.)

In many churches, the youth leader is the second most important Bible teacher after the minister. You have a week-by-week teaching ministry with those in your group. This means you have probably got more teaching responsibility even than the assistant minister, if you have one. That is quite a responsibility. But it's not always an easy one, as Tim and Linda found out . . .

It's Thursday evening and Tim and Linda sit down to prepare the youth group for the coming Sunday. They haven't been doing it for long, and to be honest they'd rather not be doing it now. But they were asked by the vicar, and then morally pummelled into it with the well-tried 'If you can't do it, I'm not sure there's anyone else.'

Still, it's not as bad as they'd thought it would be. The members are amiable. Their parents are appreciative. There's a good atmosphere in the group, and everyone enjoys the Sunday evenings. There are even some good resources around to help Tim and Linda in their weekly preparation.

Just at the moment they're religiously working through a new booklet on Old Testament characters which they picked up at the local Christian bookshop. This booklet is great. It suggests all sorts of games and activities and tells you what to say about the characters concerned. All you have to do is simply work through it, exercise by exercise, page by page.

In fact, Tim jokes to Linda, they needn't turn up at all, just give the booklet to one of the older members to read out at each meeting. And Linda begins to think, 'Well maybe that's not such a bad idea . . . After all we've got to be away in two weeks' time and there's no one to take the group for us then.'

So it's all going pretty well at the moment. But Tim and Linda have a nagging doubt: 'In six months' time we'll have used all the published resources we know about. What then? Get out while the going's good? Hand over to someone else? Slowly sink beneath the rising storm of the kids' boredom?'

What happens when Tim and Linda's current 'super resource' runs out? There are other things around, but they don't seem quite so well suited to the group. Are they going to be able to use them? Linda's been thinking 'I suppose we could adapt them, but I'm really not too sure how'.

This book is for Tim and Linda. And for you if you are a youth leader. It is specifically aimed to help you as you think about and prepare the main teaching sessions for your youth group. You can use it as yet another book from which to raid good ideas. But I hope it will do more for you than this. I want to explore how we can understand the Bible for ourselves, so that we can be more effective youth group leaders and teachers. I want to show you how to create your own ideas, resources and teaching programmes.

I'm making big assumptions about the aims of Christian youth work and about the methods we use. These are covered later in this chapter. For the moment, I'm assuming that you want to teach your young people about God, and that you have a regular time in which you aim to do this.

There are huge areas of youth ministry which are not covered in this book. You won't find anything specifically on social activities for youth groups, holiday ideas or youth work specifically with the disadvantaged. And you won't find much about the principles of Christian youth work, or stunning examples of how one youth leader has overcome inconceivable difficulties in building up her youth group. This is a book about communicating the truth about God to young people.

So if you're serious about doing that, read on.

The Creative Ladder

All youth leaders are somewhere on the 'creative ladder'. We all start somewhere near the bottom, and through experience and learning make some progress towards the top.

At the bottom end, people are totally dependent on published resources. They plug into these, follow every detail, and do precisely what the published resource tells them to do.

At the top end, people don't use *any* published resources. They start with a blank sheet of paper, dream up scintillating games and activities without any difficulty at all, and are able to teach their young people in such a way that they are entertained, informed and challenged all at the same time.

Don't worry, most youth leaders never get anywhere near the top!

But we can all progress some way up from the bottom.

Adaptation – a possibility

For many of us, when we buy a book of games we put on a straitjacket. We feel we have to use them. And we have to use them just as the book says we should.

Nonsense! Any published resource can be adapted. And all published material will probably contain things which are poor, inept, irrelevant or unusable in your group. So we need to select and adapt, selecting the usable from the unusable, and then adapt the usable to our particular situation.

And we can all do that. One of the aims of this book is to help in this task.

Originality – a possibility

Further up this 'creative ladder', some youth leaders may want to think up their own ideas, or use something which caught their eye whilst watching TV last night. That sort of thing is not only for the select few. We can all begin to develop original ideas.

Understanding – a possibility

Others will be growing in their understanding of Bible passages, and will be developing the ability critically to assess the contributions of commentaries and other resources. Again, that's a possibility for all of us.

From dependence to independence

When you move up this 'creative ladder', you move from dependence to independence. It is a growth from dependence on published resources to an independence from them. You continue to use the available resources, but are not bound by them.

A useful analogy is with Third World countries. In times of crisis, developed countries can help those in the developing world by providing food. Or they can offer more long-term help through programmes which help Third World farmers to develop and use their own agriculture. Gradually they will become self-sufficient.

In the same way, if youth leaders can develop their own teaching evenings and stand more on their own two feet, then that it progress. And it should mean that members learn more on these occasions.

Of course this is only useful if the group do not 'starve' in the meantime. So there are also examples of youth group teaching evenings in the 'Key Example' section of each chapter. The purpose of these is twofold. First, to give examples of how the principles outlined work out in practice. Second, to suggest material which you can use with your group.

How to use this book

It will seem tempting at this point to turn straight to the examples and use the first of them next week, ignoring the rest of the book.

That might turn out to be a short-sighted and ultimately pointless exercise. It will not necessarily make you a better youth leader.

Please read the rest of the book, think about it, talk with other leaders about it, look at the examples. And then be bold. Try out a few new things. Step into uncharted territory.

Jumping the gun

Let's not jump the gun and talk about the 'how?' before being clear on the 'what?' and the 'why?'

We have a responsibility as Christian youth leaders to tell our young people about God, and in particular what God has done for us in Jesus Christ. It is this spiritual element which marks out Christian youth work from secular youth work. This is not to run down secular youth work. There is much that we can learn from those involved in this area. But this book is not an encyclopedia: my focus is Christian teaching.

We want young people to learn about God and what he has done for us in Jesus Christ. The information they need comes supremely from the Bible. Christian youth leaders are Bible teachers; the Bible is our text book. This does not mean that we stand in front of the group week by week with a piece of chalk in our hand as may have been the case in the past. The New

Testament idea of teaching is far broader than this and emphasises, for example, life to life communication and a deep commitment to a few people.

The key point is that when we get together for the 'serious session' of the week we will, in one way or another, teach the Bible to our young people.

Aiming high

Aims are long term and fairly general by nature. They answer the questions 'What am I trying to *do* with my group?', and 'What do we want to achieve?'

Youth work is one of those areas where it's very easy not to think very carefully, if at all. Colossians 1:28 is a very important Bible verse for outlining aims for youth work: 'We proclaim Jesus, admonishing and teaching everyone with all wisdom, so that we may present everyone perfect in Christ.'

Our aims are as long term as they can be. The end in sight is presenting members of our youth groups to Jesus Christ when he returns, or when they die – whichever happens first.

The aim which Paul had for the Colossian Christians was that they would be 'perfect in Christ'. Another Bible translation reads, 'mature in Christ'. So, for our current youth group, our aim is that we should be working hard to help Simon, Russ, Jenny, Neil, Rachel and the rest to grow to Christian maturity, so that when Jesus returns we will be able to present them to him, 'perfect in Christ'.

Of course that involves young people becoming Christians first, and then going on growing as Christians. This involves a long term view, and seeing youth work in the context of the work of the rest of the church in the rest of their lives.

Methods of youth work

If our aim is to teach young people so that they grow towards Christian maturity, how do we bring that about?

Look again at Colossians 1:28 where Paul talks about 'proclaiming him' (that's Jesus Christ), 'admonishing and teaching everyone with all wisdom'.

If Paul's aim is to be ours, then it is essential that we focus on teaching the Bible, whether through up-front teaching, late-night discussions, or living a life among our young people which is daily moulded by the Scriptures. The Bible points to and focuses on Jesus Christ; he is its subject. And Christians without Christ can never mature. It makes sense therefore to use the Bible to proclaim Jesus to our groups. The negative 'admonishing' and positive 'teaching' are also best achieved by simply teaching the Bible.

> I could continue to list the benefits of regular scriptural reading, but why should I? The living God has spoken. The ruler of the universe has revealed himself in print. Yet still we hesitate. Why? (John White, *Hear the Word*.)

Evangelism or discipling?

Whether it be evangelism or discipling, teaching the Bible is fundamental. In fact, our job is precisely the same in both. Evangelism and discipling are defined by the hearer and not by the speaker. If you're teaching the Bible to non-Christians, it is evangelism. If you're teaching it to Christians, it is discipling – whatever the passage.

This leads to an interesting question relating to Jesus and the disciples. When was he 'evangelising' them and when was he 'discipling' them? It is hard to say. We cannot say when they became Christians, and for many in our youth groups we cannot say for sure either.

I became a Christian through a church youth group, but I do not know exactly when it was. The speakers at our group during my six months' transition from pagan to Christian were speaking to someone who might, or might not, have been a Christian. They may have been involved in evangelism or in discipling. They do not know, and nor do I. And it does not matter. They were doing the important thing; they were teaching me the Bible.

Feeding sheep

There are plenty of other Bible references to the need to be teaching the Bible to our groups. In 1 Peter 5:2 Peter commands

the elders (and I take youth leaders to be biblically part of this role
in the church), 'Be shepherds of God's flock that is under your
care.' Shepherds can and do carry out a number of tasks for the
sheep. The most important is feeding them, or to be more precise,
leading them to pasture. It is particularly striking that when Jesus
reinstated Peter (John 21:15–19) his response to Peter's claim to
love Jesus was, 'Feed my lambs', 'Take care of my sheep', and
'Feed my sheep'. The primary task of a leader is to feed those he or
she leads; youth leaders need to feed their groups. And this is best
done by teaching them the Bible.

> The Bible plays a central and utterly vital role in Christian ministry
> with youth . . . Youth must come to grips with God's word as his
> revelation of reality, and learn to act on it. (Lawrence O. Richards,
> *Youth Ministry – It's Renewal in the Local Church*.)

Staying with Peter, we see in 1 Peter 2:2 the command, 'Like new
born babies, crave pure spiritual milk, so that by it you may grow
up in your salvation.' Seen in the context of the preceding verses
this is referring to the word of the Lord which is living and
enduring: 'For you have been born again not of perishable seed
but of imperishable, through the living and enduring word of
God' (1 Peter 1:23).

The word was also preached: 'And this is the word that was
preached to you' (1 Peter 1:25). So the original readers and hearers
of Peter's first letter heard the word of God preached, they were
born again as a result of this, and were to grow by feeding on the
word of God. The same is true of us.

> God's word is as essential to us spiritually as food is to us physically
> . . . It is by his word that God implants spiritual life within us. (John
> Stott, *Understanding the Bible*.)

The apostle Peter knew the importance of God's word for
spiritual growth. In 1 and 2 Timothy, Paul stresses to Timothy the
need to continue to teach and preach the word of God.

> Preach the word; be prepared in season and out of season; correct,
> rebuke and encourage with great patience and careful instruction
> (2 Timothy 4:2).

The Bible is full of examples of this. I have selected just a few. Teaching the Bible is *the* way in which Christian growth both numerically and in depth is achieved. But note again, teaching needs to be taken in its wider meaning. I'm not just talking about chalk and talk, but rather about using a whole range of different methods to communicate God's truth so that young people learn about Christ.

Making the Bible come alive

Now let's put our feet back on the ground. What about the teaching slot in our youth programme? For that matter, what about the Sunday sermons and mid-week study groups?

Tragically much Bible teaching is dead. It has got a bad name for itself, and to be honest that is not surprising.

There are two main reasons for this:

- **Poor Understanding.** We deprive the Bible of its power when we fail to understand it. So often we do not dig deeply enough, or simply use it as a quarry from which to build our own ideas.
- **Poor presentation.** Even when we've understood a particular verse or passage, it can then be made killingly boring by the way we present it to our young people. Sometimes this reflects our attitudes. Sometimes it reflects poor preparation. Sometimes it is the result of sheer lack of experience.

Understanding and presentation: these are the keys. And working on these areas is the aim of this book.

Many youth leaders recognise their limitations when it comes to presentation. If only, they say, I could think of new games and exciting visual aids. Of course, it's good to have lively presentation ideas. But these need to be seen in perspective. There is nothing more creative or powerful and more interesting than the Bible, imaginatively explained. Presentation ideas don't harm: they can help young people overcome their natural prejudice against the Bible, and they can help brilliantly in young people's learning. But nothing is more stimulating than the Bible itself.

In a nutshell: good understanding is vital, good presentation is helpful.

I want to show how important it is to have a clear understanding of the passage we are teaching, and how this is possible for all of us. Understanding the Bible correctly is the vital first step. With good, clear understanding of the Bible and good presentation, we are on to a winner. The Bible will be seen as it truly is – *alive*.

Life to life

Young people learn enormous amounts from other people. Over a period of time they soak up things like a sponge from other young people and from older people such as their youth leaders. They learn the values and lifestyle of those around them. As youth leaders, we want to teach our young people a lifestyle, and the best possible method of teaching a lifestyle is to live it out alongside them. That means they have got to see us regularly, and not for just two hours on a Sunday evening. They must see us living out the Christian life in particular situations alongside them. This is the way Jesus worked with the twelve disciples. This is the way my youth leader, through whom I became a Christian, worked with me. I don't remember much of what he taught us in the group meetings, but I do remember things like the way he always had a Bible in his car, and verse cards in his loo. I recall the way he would always be up early to read his Bible and pray. No matter how good our teaching techniques, they would all be rather hollow if the Gospel is not lived out alongside our group members.

Christianity is best communicated from an older Christian life to a younger or non-Christian life.

Bible Teachers in Context

Youth teaching differs from teaching in a pulpit; our young people know us for what we are; we live out our Christian lives among them and they measure our Bible teaching against what they see in our lives.

It's life to life

The Christian faith is not just a series of propositions which we can mentally tick off. It's a whole lifestyle.

The best way of communicating the Christian faith is from one life to another. In our case it is from an older Christian life to a younger or non-Christian life. Formal times of Bible teaching are important, but these must be set in the context of opportunities for young people to see how it works out in practice. That means that we must build into our programmes time to be with our young people doing ordinary things, so that they can get to know us, and we them. We do not need more meetings, but more informal situations, where young people can see how the Christian faith works out in practice.

This means that our programmes will allow for social evenings, outings and the like. But we also need to give time to informal opportunities to develop friendships with those in our groups. One of the lads in our current youth group helped me lay our back lawn and patio, came to a wedding with us just recently, uses my computer, and is always sitting in our kitchen drinking tea. We are good friends. And the Christian faith is being communicated from one life to another.

It's example

> The youth leader is not primarily a talker or organiser. He is a model, a person who by the power of his own Christian example motivates dedication to Jesus Christ (Lawrence O. Richards, *Youth Ministry – Its Renewal in the Local Church*.)

With this exposure of our lives to those of our young people, our consistent example is important. But to leave it there would result in a severe outbreak of paranoia.

The most important times of learning are very often when we botch it up and our young people see us at our worst. Jesus let his disciples see him weak, vulnerable and in pain. By contrast we like to maintain the image of the superhero youth leader. But when we let ourselves and God down, and then make amends, we are giving a powerful example to our young people.

When I let my impatience show, when I'm a hopeless husband and father, and then try to improve, my example is powerful. As Paul wrote in 1 Timothy 4:15, 'Be diligent in these matters; give yourself wholly to them, so that everyone may see your progress'. He was not urging Timothy to be better than others, but to *be better than he was*.

It's long term work with a few

This life to life communication is not just a two-week affair. This is a deep, long-term commitment. To a few.

You cannot hope to help significantly more than a handful of young people. You may try, but you will not be able to work deeply with more than three or four.

Jesus's way of working was always to focus his ministry. He neglected vast areas of service in order to concentrate on working with twelve people. Of those twelve, he concentrated on Peter, James and John.

But this focusing of ministry was not peculiar to Jesus. It appears throughout the New Testament. The early church discerned those in whom God was at work. And that is precisely our role today. We look for those in whom God is working and then work alongside him with those people.

This means you will be looking for:

- **Multiple Leadership,** as each leader works with a few people.
- **Discernment,** as you decide specifically with whom you will work.
- **Organisation,** as you divide the group between the leaders.
- **Prayerfulness,** as you pray in detail for those you know well.

How long do you think you will lead your youth group for? If the principles outlined above are right, then a three year commitment to being a youth leader is probably the absolute minimum. Contemporary youth culture would have us believe in instant results. Spiritual work among the young may move faster than among the old, but we are still talking of growing oak trees, not beansprouts.

It's invisible

Much youth work is driven by images of contemporary youth culture, and as a result success is judged purely by numbers, atmosphere and response.

The Bible never equates success with any of these criteria. God usually works in unseen ways, and his greatest, most powerful acts are often those which appear weak and insignificant.

Perhaps the worst question that any church member can ask of a youth leader is, 'How many came last night?' It either induces guilt or feelings of success. Yet success in youth work or in any other area of the Christian life is to be judged according to our obedience to God's will in the way it is done. That may well result in increased numbers. But it may not. Low numbers don't necessarily mean failure. Numerical growth is not necessarily a sign of success.

Teaching the Bible may not seem to produce spectacular results, but our goal is to change lives long-term, which may or may not produce dramatic impact initially. There may be other areas that we can improve to increase the size of our group, but we should not give up doing this one central task however large or small our group is. There will be a great temptation to change methods, to make it all more 'attractive' and 'relevant'. People, especially other youth leaders, will put unintentional pressure on us to change our ways.

But we are Bible teachers. It may not be spectacular on earth. It will certainly be spectacular in heaven.

Before You Read On ✳

The aim of this book is to help you be slightly better youth leaders, by being slightly better Bible teachers.

Maybe you haven't yet started teaching the Bible to your group. I hope you will.

Maybe you do, but are firmly tied to published resources.

Maybe you're outstandingly brilliant and creative.

Wherever you are, I hope this book makes your task a little easier.

When we see God speaking to our young people as we teach the Bible, that's just about the most exciting thing on earth.

This suggested an exercise to do - As it starts it says before you read on..."read on".

2

Spoiled for choice –
Ways of communicating the Bible
to Young People

It's Sunday evening, 8.00 pm.

The youth group at St Jemima's are just beginning to turn up at the church hall for an evening on 'The media'. They begin with a few songs, led with an out-of-tune guitar by a leader who thought of the songs during the sermon at church that evening. His co-leader then takes over and gives a twenty-minute talk about the evils of broadcasting and journalism. Most of the youth group have already been to church that evening, so this is their second sermon within the hour. Most drift into thinking about the day at school tomorrow, the girl in the row in front, their best friend's new boyfriend, that new pair of jeans . . . After the meeting there is coffee, but people soon drift off. Later when one is asked by his mum what the youth group was about this evening, he replies, vaguely, 'Sex, I think,' and then heads for the TV.

Across the other side of town, Heathfield Independent Youth Group have also arranged an evening on 'The media'. As the members arrive at the leader's home, and have coffee and cake (it's one of the girl's birthdays), they jot down their offerings on a graffiti board headed 'My favourite TV programme.' When the meeting gets under way, one of the leaders shows the results of the survey she and two group members conducted on Saturday afternoon.

They had borrowed a video camera and asked people in the town centre what their favourite TV programmes were. The results were hilarious. As the evening continues, the members fill in a media consumption review for the past week, and are staggered by how much of the media they consume in just one week. One of the leaders talks about the dangers and the positive aspects of the media. She illustrates this with snippets from adverts and soap operas recorded the previous week by one of the group members. Then they go into groups to look at Philippians 4:8–20, and see what attitude the Christian should have towards the media. She concludes with the phrase 'The media – watch it with your eyes open', which becomes a bit of a catch phrase around the group for the next couple of months.

Neither of these two methods of teaching the same subject are wrong. There are groups (and leaders!) for whom the Heathfield Independent Church method would be totally inappropriate. In this chapter we will see the variety of possible methods of teaching the Bible, and think about what some people call 'active learning'. Remember that throughout Scripture the *content* of what is said is more important than the method of communication.

So, for us, our message is more important than our methods. We must not let our methods rule our message. That is why chapters 3 and 4 on getting our message right are so important. What we say is the most important aspect of our teaching. This is fundamental.

When we know the content we can choose appropriate methods to communicate it in the best possible way.

Our choice of methods therefore depends on the message itself, the hearers, and the circumstances in which the teaching takes place.

Some things are best taught by straight talk, some by a group Bible study, others by activities such as games. This chapter, and chapter 5, will help you to decide which methods to use when.

Jesus used methods such as asking questions to check understanding (eg Mark 8:27, 'Who do people say I am?') and on-the-job learning (eg Luke 9:2, 'And he sent them out to preach the kingdom of God and heal the sick').

Jesus was canny (not always giving straight answers), visual and humorous. He used poetry (the Beatitudes), and arguments. He was keen on learning by doing, and so tells the rich young man to sell his possessions:

> 'If you want to be perfect, go, sell your possessions and give to the poor, and you will have treasure in heaven. Then come, follow Me' (Matthew 19:21).

Jesus tailored his method to the people he was working with. He used Scripture with those who were used to it, but common sense and everyday conversation with those who were not.

Could be expanded.

And it is not only Jesus. In the Old Testament, the Passover is used as a teaching medium. Hosea uses his marriage as an illustration of the relationship between Israel and God, and Nathan uses a case study to reveal David's sin to him (2 Samuel 12:1–15).

Active Learning – why?

Active learning is the 'hands-on' approach: learning by doing, as well as by seeing and hearing. Why should we encourage 'active learning'?

Because of the way we learn

You can learn about wind-surfing from a book. But you need to get on the board and do it in order to learn and remember for next time. It may be uncomfortable, cold and wet, but it is the only way to learn. Being involved means you learn more easily because it stimulates many different parts of your personality. All the senses are involved: hearing, seeing, touching, sensing. Your body is involved: feeling wet and cold and tired. And it also impinges on your emotions: fear, excitement, anger, depression! Involvement helps learning.

Remember, too, that people cannot concentrate for very long. When my wife was at college, one of her lecturers would talk only for twenty minutes and then take a break before another twenty minute session. He knew that the students could not concentrate for more than twenty minutes. For youth groups, that time span is likely to be far less. We all concentrate best in short bursts, and therefore learn best in short bursts. So we need to keep our programme moving, and limit each part to a 'bite-sized chunk'.

If something is learned by doing it, it is far more likely to be remembered than if it's learned by seeing. And since learning is not just about understanding, but also memory and action, that is important.

People quote statistics about this: after three weeks you only retain 10% of what you see, 5% of what you hear, and 3% of what you read. But you remember 70% of what you do.

Because of the young people

What is it about our young people that makes them more suitable for active learning than, say, older people?

Today's young people are not conditioned to learning from monologue. They do not know how to concentrate on one person speaking to them for any length of time.

In our churches, though, talks are still important, and many of the young people who have been brought up within churches have developed the ability to learn from monologue. Non-Christian young people often do not have this ability and, by relying on 'the talk', we are cutting ourselves off from the rest of the world. Activity-based learning will help non-Christians to learn and feel more at home in our groups. Today's teenagers *are* used to modern educational methods at school. They will feel more at home with them than we do. (But that does not mean that our youth group evenings become like school!)

Young people should enjoy our youth meetings and active learning is fun. They may well enjoy them because their boyfriend (or potential boyfriend) is there, or because they enjoy making a fool of themselves. Playing occasional games is fun, and also teaches things which they remember.

Because of the group

Think for a moment about your group, about the variety of people in it and their different needs. We are all different. Some learn quickly, others slowly (or not at all!). Some have good memories, some hopeless. Some understand instructions quickly, others very slowly. Some can think about abstract things such as love and justice; others are more concrete in their thinking. If we try to communicate with all those different people by giving a talk, we and our members are likely to come away with a big headache.

But if we use active learning methods, everyone has more of a chance to learn at their own level.

20 Ways to Teach

1 Straight talk

Good for
- Evangelistic meetings
- A change from your regular diet of activities
- Easier to prepare

Watch
- You'll probably need audiovisual aids which take extra time to prepare
- Use it for a change and not because you don't have time to find good activities
- Make one point well and don't go on for too long. Stop while they still want more

Try
- Involving your group in your preparation

2 Role play

Good for
- A bit of fun
- Initiating discussion
- Looking at problems from others' viewpoint
- Improving acting ability!

Watch
- Make sure people feel safe to join in – an ice-breaker would help here
- Explain the situation clearly
- People can get very emotionally involved so de-role them afterwards into their real characters
- Give a time limit

Try
- Giving a first or last line, (eg 'I'll tell your Mum'), and getting members to improvise

- Giving members an outline to their character with blanks to personalise it
- Giving members a prop or phrase they have to say
- Giving members the first half of a biblical account and ask them to finish it
- Playing Ananias persuading the other Christians that Saul really has become a Christian
- Acting in pairs or one large group – a fish bowl – where some role play and others watch

Role play

This is where members play themselves in different situations or take on a whole new character. They are good for a bit of fun, for initiating discussion, for looking at the problem from others' viewpoints, and for improving acting ability!

If you're using a role play, make sure people know each other and are relaxed in each other's company. Young people tend not to like the idea of role play until they actually do it. So don't introduce it by saying 'We're going to do a role play'. Be more subtle than that. You may need to use a good ice-breaker first so that everyone feels safe joining in. Role plays require a fair bit of preparation and can be handled in a number of ways. For example, you can give a first or a last line (eg 'They're due any moment', 'You'll be late for school', etc), or give people an outline of their character with blanks to add in their own ideas.

Try playing out a biblical situation as if they were there. Give the group the first half of a biblical account, and then ask them to finish. Then get them to look it up and see how it does finish.

Role plays can be short and sweet (eg in pairs, A talks to B, but B doesn't listen, then B talks to A, but A butts in all the time), or longer (eg simulate a staff meeting at school).

Make sure you explain the situation clearly and give a time limit (or end point – for example, when someone says, 'In which case I'll tell the Bishop'). Get people familiar with their new names by getting them to say them out loud and de-role at the end by getting them to say who they really are.

Role plays can be used to good effect in practical training. For example, someone calls you to say they will not be coming to the group any more because their mum says that Christianity is all lies. In pairs, act out the 'phone call. Or act a role play of you in the group when you have just heard that X has been arrested for possession of drugs. Or act out how the present group would react if a law had been passed to ban smoking.

A variant on this is the fish bowl, where a small number of people either do a role play, or another activity, and are observed by the rest of the group, who then report back. This can be useful, especially with very shy people, who would freeze in a role play, or if you have a very large group and a small number of leaders.

Role plays: lots of potential, but handle with care. Remember to debrief fully.

3 Audio visual aids

Good for
- Making a big impression
- Raising interest, introducing humour
- Aiding long-oterm memory

Watch
- Use as your servant, not your master
- The time it takes to prepare them
- Displaying them for so long that they distract from what you're saying

Try
- Clip art books
- Buying an overhead projector (and count it as part of your giving!)
- Getting an artistic group or church members to prepare your visual aids

4 TV/radio/photography/video

Good for
- Variety
- High visual impact
- Keeping up to date and relevant

Watch
- Make sure you know how to use the technology
- Don't become a slave to them
- The cost

Try
- Asking group members to record snippets for you
- Video/record the news headlines then pray for it
- If you can't be there for the group meeting, record your input on video
- Interview members during the meeting and play back the results

5 Discussion

Good for
- Memory as members verbalise their thoughts
- Involving group members
- Studying the Bible

Watch
- Avoid, 'Right, what shall we discuss tonight, then?'
- Decide how the discussion will be led, and who will lead it
- Draw out quieter ones and don't let the noisy or verbose dominate

Try
- Using AVAs to display discussion questions and instructions
- Snowball discussions – two people discuss then team up with another pair and so on
- Using video snippets for discussion starters

6 Questionnaires: interview friends, group members, strangers...

Good for
- Getting the members thinking
- Up to date – keeps you informed on what young people are thinking

Watch
- Don't make them too long
- Do publish the results
- Make sure questions are clear and well thought out

Try
- A survey of feelings on sex before marriage/smoking/the Bible
- Doing it on tape or video: take a camcorder into your local High Street and ask teenagers who they think Jesus Christ was
- Involve members in conducting any questionnaire

7 Computers

Good for
- Good cheap handouts
- Small groups

Watch
- Don't intimidate other youth leaders with it
- Don't try and 'keep up with the Joneses'
- Some things are quicker by hand

Try
- Create a database of your youth group for address labels, records, etc, but keep within the Data Protection Act
- Using Christian software packages

8 Practical activity

Good for
- Practical service and training

- Evangelism
- One-to-one personal work

Watch
- Doing this sort of thing once – and never again
- Be involved yourself

Try
- Cooking a meal for/helping out older members of the church
- Door-to-door visiting in pairs (ideally one leader and one member)

9 Games

Good for
- Clear understanding
- Long-term memory
- Fun
- Members' involvement and building group atmosphere

Watch
- Time it takes
- Make sure the game teaches the point you want to teach
- Give clear instructions
- Have a good debrief (reflections, interpretation, application)
- Don't play games and nothing else

Try
- Adapt board games like Scrabble
- The pathbuilding game from chapter 4

Games

'Games' covers a very wide range of activity-based learning, and is not as frivolous as it may sound! For a detailed explanation of the valuable role of games in learning see *Everyone's a Winner* by Jim Belben and Trevor Cooper, published by Bible Society. This book also includes instructive games to teach the Bible. They work.

There are all sorts of games which can be used. Board games can be utilised, you can copy TV games (like 'Blockbusters') and radio games (like 'Just a Minute' or the old favourite '20 Questions'). Use 'Just a Minute' for subjects such as My bedroom, Washing up, Doing the housework.

It is not hard to begin to think up your own games. For example, why not have two teams, each with a tube of toothpaste, and then have a competition to see which team can leave the longest line of toothpaste. It is a useful introduction to the subject of words, which are like toothpaste, in that once they are out, you can't put them back in again.

As with all games, we must make sure that the instructions and rules are clear, and the debrief is very important. This should contain.

- reflection (how do you feel about this?)
- interpretation (what did it mean to you?)
- application (what should we do about it?)

Some say the debrief should be longer than the game. But you can overdo it, and end up with people not enjoying or learning from the game because they are dreading the debrief. It is better to have a short sharp point at the end which has been clearly demonstrated by the game.

---

10 Collages from newspapers and magazines

Good for
- Introducing a particular topic (eg, sin, war, gossip – members cut out relevant material)
- Group participation – all members are involved
- Opening eyes

Watch
- Over-enthusiasm
- Make sure you make the point from the exercise

Try
- Just cutting out headlines
- Use teenage magazines as an introduction to an evening on sex

11 Brainstorm

Good for
- Collecting a wide range of ideas quickly: members call out responses or ideas and these are listed (eg on OHP)
- Involving a lot of members
- Introducing a subject

Watch
- No comments on any contribution (especially no negative comments) until the brainstorming is over
- Make sure you refer back to it later
- One member dominating

Try
- Collecting ideas on sheets on the wall of the meeting room (eg five sheets on Ephesians 2:1–10 headed God, Sin, Non-Christians, What God has done, Why God has done it)

12 Ice-breakers

Good for
- Starting the meeting
- Relaxing people
- Making newcomers feel welcome
- Opening up cliques
- Helping strangers meet each other

Watch
- Creating an atmosphere of excessive frivolity that will make concentration difficult
- Doing the same one two weeks running

Try
- Signature Bingo (see Key Example)
- Graffiti Board (see Key Example)

13 Drama

Good for
- Involving members

- Helping members get inside a subject
- Helping long-term memory and understanding

Watch
- Imposing it on the shy and easily embarrassed
- Always the same members being involved

Try
- Asking members of your church drama group to present a sketch
- Invite a professional group to perform at your church

14 Letter writing

Good for
- Developing imagination: members put themselves into the shoes of a Bible character and write a letter expressing their thoughts and feelings (eg the centurion at Jesus' crucifixion writes home)
- Thinking more deeply about a situation
- Unwrapping narrative passages of the Bible

Watch
- It doesn't get unhelpfully speculative
- It doesn't work well on some parts of the Bible, eg letters, poetry, wisdom literature

Try
- Telemessages
- Mini-sagas to summarise the passage

15 Demonstration

Good for
- Learning practical skills: the youth leader shows how something is done and the young people do it (eg evangelism training)
- Building confidence in individuals
- Smaller groups and one-to-one work

Watch
- Make sure you can do it well before trying this
- Avoid being idolised by your young people

Try
- Demonstrating how to explain the cross
- Demonstrating how to lead someone to commitment
- Demonstrating how to welcome newcomers to the group

16 Quiet time out during meetings to think

Good for
- Individual application of a Bible passage
- Showing the seriousness of Christianity

Watch
- Assess your group first – could they cope with this? Give guidance on how to use the time
- Don't go on for too long

Try
- Focusing on one short Bible passage

17 Activity

Good for
- Serving others outside the youth group: the group actively do something during the meeting such as weeding someone's garden
- Making one point well
- Binding the group together
- Memory and enjoyment

Watch
- Time: activities always go on for longer than you think
- Confusion: make clear what you are teaching

Try
- Cooking
- Toothpaste race

18 Paraphrase a Bible passage

Good for
- Looking carefully at one Bible passage
- Learning to express Christian truth without jargon

Watch
- Changing the meaning
- Those with poor literary skills

Try
- Paraphrasing 2 Corinthians 5:21 into non-jargon. (This is very hard!)
- Story telling (members re-tell a Bible account in their own words)

19 Case study and problem solving

Good for
- Applying principles: participants have to apply the principles they have learnt to a real or imaginary situation
- Introducing the subject when looking at a topic (eg materialism)

Watch
- Time (these can be very lengthy)
- It must be realistic

Try
- Spice by getting your group to solve a *real life* case study problem. Watch confidentiality and let them know what really happened
- Problem-solving (a particular form of case study)

20 Memorising Bible verses

Good for
- Building up Bible knowlege – one verse a week soon adds up
- Recapping what you learned last time

Watch
- Those with genuinely poor memories
- Make sure it doesn't become a hollow ritual

Try
- Doing it! (it's been neglected during the last ten years or so)
- Writing up the verse in four colours on an OHP/large piece of paper. Then divide your group in four and give each a colour to shout out as you go through the verse. Chop and change, and then say it all together.

Special One

John 13 – An example of communication

Note the variety of methods that Jesus used in this one chapter. He communicated:
- **Visually** verse 4: 'So Jesus got up from the meal, took off his outer clothing, and wrapped a towel round his waist.'
- **Through activity** verse 5: 'After that he poured water into a basin and began to wash his disciples feet.'
- **Personally** verse 7: Jesus replied 'You do not realise now what I am doing, but later you will understand.'
- **Through a debrief** verse 12: 'Do you understand what I have done for you?' he asked them?
- **With a lesson** verse 14: 'Now that I, your Lord and teacher, have
  washed your feet, you also should wash one another's feet.'

How should we use these methods?

Teach the Bible

This is most important. Remember that we use all these different ideas in order to teach the Bible. Any activity must support the aim of the meeting, and the aim will be to teach the central theme of the Bible passage (see chapter 3). Of course there may be subsidiary points to be made, but do not let these oust the main aim of the meeting. Ask yourself if the particular method you have chosen is communicating the truth which you want to teach.

Don't be Mr or Ms Cool!

Join in and be enthusiastic. It will build your relationships with the group members, which is the most important way they will learn.

If you stay cool about new activities, your members will be too. Be prepared to look a fool. Be a coach and an encourager. Lead from the front saying, 'Come and do this, it will be fun', rather than, 'Go and do it, you'll enjoy it'.

Be Wise

Not all these methods are sensible or even possible for your group, so you need to choose wisely. Do not over-expose on games; we are in the serious business of teaching the Bible.

Make the point

I remember a school biology course which was based on using activity to find out for ourselves. The problem was that we never knew whether we would find out the right thing. There were always doubts in our minds as to whether we were learning the right things or the wrong things.

So, use an activity, but then say *why* you did it, and *what* you wanted to teach through it. Drive the point home. Ensure no one is in any doubt about what you are trying to get across.

Of course, it helps if it is clear in your own mind first . . .

Learn from others

When you see other youth leaders in action, or hear about other youth groups, pick up all you can from the way they do things. What's good? What's not? Why are they so effective? Do not always copy the good (it may be something about their particular personality which no-one else can copy), but do try to avoid the bad.

It is also useful to keep your eyes open for ideas all the time – as you watch TV, browse through magazines, read other people's papers on the bus, listen to the radio, visit Christian bookshops, go to training events, and so on. Keep your own book of ideas. It will come in handy some time.

A final note

A lot of these ideas are from educationalists. They are taken from the classroom. But it would be a serious mistake to model what we do with our youth groups solely on a secular education system.

We are communicating not just ideas and information but a way of life, a whole culture, a faith. And we cannot do that just in the youth group meeting once a week. That is why our own Christian faith, and the example we give, is so important. The expression of our faith in real-life situations, and seeing our faith work out in practice, is so important. Living the Christian life alongside our young people is vital and irreplaceable.

Special Two

Youth group meetings checklist

When using active learning methods we need to:
- **Be specific** Focus in on one thing to teach. Your group will probably only remember one thing from the meeting, so make sure you're the one who decides what it is!
- **Be selective** All teaching activities must focus on one point. So prune, and make sure all that is done supports this one thing we are teaching. Do not be over-ambitious.
- **Be varied** Don't do any one thing for too long. Keep moving. Move on before the members get bored. Stay one step ahead of them.
- **Be clear** Not only about what is being taught, but also about what you want the members to do, how long they've got, etc
- **Be daring** Try out new things. Stretch yourself – but make sure you practise first! Use shock tactics and intrigue. Try to be original, and think up the odd thing yourself.

Key Example 1

Growing More Like Jesus – Session 2
How Can I be Sure?

INTRODUCTION

The purpose of these key examples is twofold.

First, they show how the ideas and principles outlined in the chapter work out in practice.

Second, they give you something to use in a future youth group teaching evening.

But please don't use the example without looking at the short introductory notes first.

Warm up

The activities here may need to be tailored to the age of the group you are working with. That's why the cue phrases in the first activity may have to be lengthened accordingly.

Young people remember things like the Backbreaker, the Trust Walk and particularly the Supertruster exercise. Our responsibility is also to make sure that they remember what the point behind these memorable activities was.

Getting going

Learning Bible verses is going out of fashion, but is a most valuable resource for the youth leader. It's good to go back over previous weeks' memory verses to make sure they have stuck.

It's also possible to do this learning in many different ways in order to make it really enjoyable – see 'Memory learning' at the end of this key example.

Bible input

All the key examples have reference to 'Group Extra' sheets. These may be photocopied and given out to group members. The use of these sheets increases members' involvement, helps their thinking and stimulates their learning. But when asking group members to write things down, be aware of non-writers.

There is also the need for the leaders to use words. These are irreplaceable especially when it comes to explaining spiritual truth, and explaining the meaning behind a particular activity.

Take a break

All these games teach 'trust' and help understanding what it means to trust Jesus. But there are far too many for one evening, so select one or two which would go down well with your group.

Take action

The use of the booklet *More Like Jesus* with this resource puts material physically into the hands of group members (which is a popular technique of salesmen . . .). This use of booklets for members is great for publishers – they sell more. But it's also educationally useful for the members. But beware two problems before you take this road:

It may be hard to get members to bring their booklets each week.

If you keep these booklets for them, how like school is it all becoming?

Music

These are not just any songs. They positively back up the theme of the evening. Singing can be used to praise and worship God. It can also be used to learn about him.

THE SESSION
Aim to teach

That being a Christian is something God wants us to be sure about, and that we *can* be sure about it.

Aim that the group should

Develop a sense of security in belonging to the group, and the certainty that each member is accepted.

Theme

Trusting Jesus.

Bible input

Luke 15:1–7

Leader's check-list

Table
Blindfolds
Bibles/Luke's Gospels
Copies of *More like Jesus*
Photocopies of 'Group Extra' sheets, plus pens

Warm-up (15–20 mins)

Try one or two of these ice-breakers:

Introductions. If the group were new to each other last week, they probably haven't yet learned everybody's name. Take a few minutes to re-make the introductions. You could ask everyone to introduce the person on their left.

Another way to re-make the introductions is to encourage each person to say a little about themselves. They can refresh the group's memory, and develop what they shared the previous week by announcing four sentences beginning with the words: 'I'm . . . I still . . . I haven't . . . But last week . . .' Again, given an example: 'I'm Paul. I still live on Weir Road Estate with my mum and sister, although the cat's run away. I haven't yet flown in a helicopter. But last week I fell off the garden wall, flapping my arms.'

Note: Younger groups may need larger cue phrases, such as 'The most stupid thing I saw last week was . . .' and will find it easier if you give them one sentence at a time. It may be good, after a humorous prelude, to hint that members of the group can share a more serious thing that's happened in the week, if they wish to.

Back-breaker. Divide into pairs, and ask one of the pair to 'faint', falling slowly backward, keeping their body rigid so that their partner can catch them under the arms, stopping their fall as close to the ground as possible. See which pair shows the greatest trust in each other, and have them demonstrate to the rest. Then ask for a volunteer 'super-truster' to stand on the table while about eight people clasp hands to catch 'super-t' as they fall backwards. This needs careful supervision! Some groups will need warning not to mess about. You may like to do a trial, with the volunteer able to fall forward first – and then backwards.

Note: Most of 'Super-t's' weight falls on the second and third pairs. Also, there's no need for the pairs to clasp hands, as long as they form a cradle for 'Super-t' to fall into.

Trust-walk. Either in the same, or in different pairs (better), one is blindfolded and spun round to disorientate. The other leads on a walk that requires trust. Then reverse roles, and the second person has to walk by faith. If restricted to one room, set up an obstacle course, with tables, chairs, rugs, string, household implements, etc. Better still, devise a circuit outside (but not across main roads) with dustbins, puddles, pot-holes, kerbs.

Give out copies of 'Group Extra', and give your own examples of how you would answer Base 1. Then, in pairs (the same as in the Trust-walk, if you used it), get them to write down the answers.

Getting going (5–10 mins)

Show some of the answers from 'Group Extra', especially about how they felt. Then ask:

• Have you learned something new about trusting other people?
• How can you tell if someone can be trusted?
• How would you check whether the introductions made earlier were reliable truths?

Briefly sum up: Trusting other people, and being trusted by them, are common, everyday experiences. For example, we trust the bus-driver to take us to where the bus claims to be going, we trust the bakery not to have let impurities get into the bread. Ask for other examples. Trusting others is part of life.

Last week we learned that 'God has shown how much he loves us . . .' (revise Romans 5:8). We're going on now to ask how far we can be sure of God, and of our relationship with Him. We are asking how far we can trust Him.

Bible input (10–15 mins)

Get together in groups of three or four (split up by eye colour, shoe size, make of jeans, colour of T-shirt, or some other original method), and ask each group to read Luke 15:1–7. Then tackle the questions in Base 2 in 'Group Extra', individually, or in the groups. Finally, share answers together in groups. But don't just leave it there. Point out that in Luke 15 Jesus actually told three similar stories. We've looked at the lost sheep (verses 1–7), which wandered ignorantly. The lost coin (verses 8–10) was lost carelessly, but the lost son (verses 11–24) rebelled deliberately.

Explain that God wants us back when we've wandered away. The group could look at *More Like Jesus* page 7. Explain that the main lesson of the chapter is that God is actively on the look-out for lost people. He is eager to welcome and accept those who turn back to Him (ie repent). And when He accepts us back, He does so fully and freely, and with great joy.

Make it clear (10–15 mins)

Try staging a pre-planned argument, with one of your other leaders playing 'devil's advocate'. They will need to break in at the end of the Bible input (and not before!), with questions such as:

- Don't I need to turn over a new leaf before God will have me?
- What if I feel like wandering off again?
- God can't really be that good, can He?
- But I'm not good enough for God.

If you decide this is too difficult, or risky, then write down the 'objections', and others that you guess your group might want to ask, onto small cards, and get members of the group to choose one at random and read it out.

Whichever method you choose try to bring the group in with their own questions, or with answers. Make sure that, from this, the first basis of our assurance is clarified: God wants us home with Him, and is actively on the look-out for lost people. 'God really wants you' – this is the first ground for being sure you are a Christian. Another is 'Facts can be trusted'.

Split your group into three's, and ask them to list facts about Jesus and His Father which they think are important and can be trusted. Brainstorm these onto on overhead projector, or large sheet of paper, and then either turn your group to *More Like Jesus*, page 6 (left-hand column), and ask them to read it, or else make sure that they have covered the five facts mentioned there: 1. Jesus is God's Son; 2. Jesus died and was raised again; 3. God wants us; 4. Jesus died for us; 5. the Holy Spirit is with us.

Take a break (5–10 mins)

Take a break now to have some refreshments. Do you keep a small supply of cola, sweets, crisps to sell? If so, tell them that paying next week stretches your trust in them too far!

Try another 'trust' game, by asking for one or more volunteers, and then blindfolding them, and feeding them with all sorts of selected delicacies, which you produce after they have been blindfolded. As you do this, lead the members of your group in all sorts of 'yah', 'ooh' type noises. See how far the blindfolded people trust you, and be sure to make the point of the importance of trusting, once you have finished.

Personal output (5–10 mins)

Restart by summarising the ground covered so far: God wants us to be sure of our relationship with Him, and we can be sure because of the two great facts of God's love for us, and Christ's work in forgiving us. These are facts that can be trusted, however we feel, and whatever the weather.

Ask your group to look at 'Free Life Assurance' ('Group Extra', base 3). Get them to fill in their coupons, and then discuss their answers. Stress the difference between what we can be sure of, as Christians, and what we can't. In this, and the next section, we look at further reassuring evidence; the Holy Spirit's work in others and in me.

First, in others: You may like to read the right-hand side of page 5 of *More Like Jesus*, or ask your group how many Christians they know. Get them to name some. Say that this is evidence of God's work, as the Holy Spirit works in others' lives. You may have someone in the group who would say how they became a Christian.

Take action (5–10 mins)

The second (and more personal) area of the Holy Spirit's work is in *me*. You could introduce this final section by looking together at *More Like Jesus*, page 6, or else give some examples of the way the Holy Spirit works in the lives of Christians. Give personal examples. Ask other leaders to illustrate in ordinary ways from their lives.

Ask your members (individually) to fill in 'Group Extra' Base 4, and then close in prayer, based around the answers to Base 4, and encourage them to pray each day this coming week about what they have written there, thanking God, and asking for His help.

Note: This may reveal significant problems which group members are facing – be sure to follow these up sensitively after the session, if necessary.

Footnotes

Memory verse. Revise Romans 5:8 from last time, and then learn together John 6:37 – 'Everyone whom my Father gives me will come to me. I will never turn away anyone who comes to me.'

Leaders' summary. We can be absolutely sure that we are Christians, that God has accepted us. We can be so sure because it was God who started to look for us, not us who started to look for Him, so He must really want us; and because the facts of the gospel (as in the Bible) and the facts of God's working in our lives and others' can be relied on.

Music. With a group which doesn't mind singing together, try these during the break, or at the beginning, or at the end:

Amazing Grace	LP 6 / MP 10 / HF 4(10) / SLW 5
Do not be worried and upset	MP 42
How good is the God we adore	MP 77
Now I belong to Jesus	MP 121

Jargon. In general, try to avoid it, but sometimes it is useful, or unavoidable. In such circumstances, *explain it*. Say, for example, at the end of the 'Bible Input' section, the word 'repent' was used. Young Christians ought to know what such words mean, but avoid positively encouraging the use of them! So, if you find yourself using such a word, be sure to re-phrase it, as well, so all can understand. In this example, 'repent' means to turn away from selfish and self-centred activities and wants, and to turn to Jesus. The 'from' and the 'to' are both important.

Memory learning. There is plenty of encouragement in the Bible for Christians to learn verses by heart – 'I have hidden your Word in my heart that I might not sin against you' (Psalm 119:11). It is not difficult, nor need it be boring. Teenagers often find it easier to memorise verses than adults. Revise the verses constantly, or they will not get into the members' long-term memory. Try to make the exercise as lively as possible – with duels, or TV-type quizzes, like 'The Verse is Right', 'Masterverse', or 'Verse Busters'. Many songs that use quotations from the Bible are an excellent way of

PHOTOCOPY THESE TWO PAGES   BACK TO BACK AND FOLD.   PAGE 1

GROUP · EXTRA

Growing more Like Jesus

HOW CAN I BE SURE ?

ARE YOU A SUPER-TRUSTER?

① When I had to fall backwards into someone else's arms, I felt...

② The worst moment for me was...

③ Having someone else rely so much on me felt...

PAGE 4.

CHECK UP

These are the ways I can already see Jesus changing me

....

....

These are the changes I would like Jesus to make in me

....

....

This is what I plan to do to help him

....

....

REMEMBER

EVERYONE WHOM MY FATHER GIVES ME WILL COME TO ME. I WILL NEVER TURN AWAY ANYONE WHO COMES TO ME.

— John 6:37

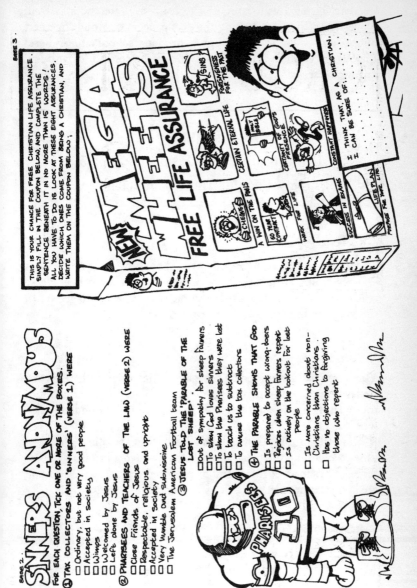

learning verses, but it is helpful to learn the references as well. Never learn them by making the group say it out loud together, unless you want to encourage a primary school atmosphere! Encourage them to learn in pairs during the session, or at home during the week.

Key Example 2
Growing More Like Jesus – Session 5
How Should I Talk About Jesus?

INTRODUCTION

The following are a few comments to show how some of the ideas and principles outlined in this chapter work out in practice. Please read them before you use the example with your youth group. In the long run they may prove helpful.

Warm up

This contains a number of fun games, but each with the same underlining theme – that of 'good news'. This helps to introduce the evening's teaching and will focus members' minds on this whole area.

Note the timing. Games take a lot of time, so allow plenty of time in planning the programme. Do not have more than two or three games in an evening, and be prepared to cut them out if you are behind schedule.

Getting going

Note the importance of reviewing past sessions. This not only cements lessons learned then, but also puts the current week's meeting in context.

Bible input

Discussion is an important learning tool. But it usually needs firm leadership and good guidance. Give good clear instructions, and if you have sufficient leaders make sure there's one for each discussion group. Also, vary the size of small groups. Always breaking into pairs or groups of four is predictable and tends to boredom. Try to vary it.

Take a break

Young people have a short concentration span. Keep things moving. Don't do any one activity for too long. A sensible rule of thumb for young people's concentration span is, 'It's usually less than you think'.

Personal output

Note the use of role play here and the reference to it in the footnotes. One point worthy of particular mention is the value of stopping early. Don't let it go on too long. It is better to stop with ten people frustrated than one bored.

Take action

When asking for the young people's opinion of various Gospel booklets, we're involving them and respecting their opinions. Very often we are bad at valuing young people's thoughts and ideas. They often have valuable insights.

THE SESSION
Aim to teach

That we need to understand what to say about Jesus, how to say it, and who to say it to.

Aim that your group should

Gain the confidence to speak naturally about Jesus to each other, and then to their friends.

Theme

Good News

Bible input

Luke 24:36–53

Leader's checklist

Packs of playing cards and prizes
Voting papers
Mars bar
Furniture
People ready for role-play
Evangelistic booklets
Re-arranged newspapers
Good News chocolates
Bibles/Luke's Gospels
Copies of *More Like Jesus*
Photocopies of 'Group Extra' sheets, plus pens

Warm up (10–15 mins)

House-builder. Divide your group into fours, and give each four a pack of playing cards, and challenge them to build the biggest card house in four minutes. (If the group is small, do this in pairs.) Award a prize (one Smartie each? or toss an open tube of Smarties to them?).

Bad news / Good news. Tell the group you have got some bad news and some good news; which would they like to hear first?

The bad news: Three people in the group are about to get 'bumped'.

The good news: One person is going to win a Mars bar.

But ask them first to try to find a person whose birthday is nearest theirs (forgetting the year), and to calculate how many days apart they are. Select the four couples whose birthdays are nearest. Tell them that there is going to be a debate. One member of each pair is in an overloaded balloon. The other member has to argue the case why their partner should *not* be thrown out. Give them two minutes to decide who will be which, and to prepare their case. Meanwhile, the rest of the group arranges a table for the four balloonists, a platform for the debaters, and seating and voting papers for themselves. Allow each debater one minute to make their case, standing on one leg, as they speak (don't warn them of this until the debate starts). Collect in the voting papers. Announce the results dramatically, one at a time – 'The bad news is that . . .!' (the group may like to 'bump' each loser). And 'The good news is that . . . wins a Mars bar!' Make sure that everyone has worked out the connection with the good/bad news and explain that this weeks' session is about sharing the good news of Jesus Christ.

Getting going (3–5 mins)

In the original pairs, tackle the questions from 'Group Extra', base 1, or handle as a quick group discussion. Sing (about the gospel being good news) at this point, if your group sings (see Footnotes).

Say that, so far, we have looked at how we can come to Jesus, how we can be sure we belong to Him, how we can listen to God from the Bible, and how we can pray. This week we'll tackle how we can tell the good news about Jesus to other people. Let's look at what Jesus said to his disciples just before He went back to heaven.

Bible input (10–15 mins)

Put three pairs together, if you have sufficient people, and, in these groups of six, read Luke 24:36–53. Discuss and answer the questions from 'Group Extra' base 2, including the Rating Chart.

Back as a whole group, explain that, unlike the balloon debate, Jesus is not asking us to win arguments for Him, but just to tell others what He means to us, and to let it appear in every part of our lives. We are not claiming that we are better than other people, but that Jesus is a friend and Saviour, who even loves people as bad as us (remember Romans 5:8). Our message is Jesus (see Luke 24:39 – 'He is alive!'), and His cross (see Luke 24:47 – 'Now everyone can be forgiven!'). Surely that is *good* news.

Turn your group to 'More Like Jesus', pages 22 and 23. Back in the pairs, get the group to read through this together, filling in the Bible references. Or, explain briefly some of the different ways of telling our friends about Jesus (eg. tell your friends how you became a Christian, look out for opportunities to give away a Christian leaflet, ask someone to a Christian event, ask God for opportunities to tell your friends what you do on Sundays, or to put a Christian viewpoint in a discussion, etc.). Then ask them to look up 1 Peter 3:15, and answer 'What must I always be ready to do?'; and Matthew 28:20, and answer 'What does Jesus promise, as we work for Him?'

Make it clear (5–10 mins)

Turn to pages 32 and 33 in 'More Like Jesus'. Ask them to fill these in individually, then to join in pairs to compare their stories. Suggest they help each other to make their stories clearer.

Alternatively, ask them to write out/work out their own story about coming to know Jesus, so they would know what to say if a friend asked 'How did you become a Christian?'. Their story (or testimony, or life-line, or some other suitable title) might have sections, covering 'before I knew Jesus', 'the thing that attracted me to Jesus', and 'now that I know Him'.

Now use base 3 from the 'Group Extra' sheet, either individually writing in the answers, or together arriving at group answers. Discuss the answers in the group. Show them that some answers are more helpful to the questioner, and some are less helpful. Show the value of a simple, brief answer, pointing to Jesus. (eg 'Why do you believe in God?' 'Because of Jesus') You could split into pairs, with one playing the non-Christian, asking the questions, and the other giving the answers. Or, if you have a smaller group, ask one of the leaders to play the non-Christian, with the whole group trying to answer their questions).

Take a break (5–10 mins)

Walk about, have coffee/Coke, crisps, sing, yawn, stretch, or play the Newspaper Game:

Have pairs sit facing each other, knees touch, shoulder to shoulder, with the next pair, as close as possible. Give each pair a large-format newspaper in which you have re-arranged the pages completely. When told, they must put the newspapers back in order: first pair gets first choice from the box of 'Good News'.

You could then start a race for the first person to thread themselves through a hole in a single sheet of newspaper. To make it more fun, you could introduce tabloid-size newspapers at this stage!

Personal output (10–15 mins)

Explain that we share Jesus by our actions, as well as our words. The more we let Him control our lives, the more other people will be made aware of Him. For some people, our actions are much better than our words: a son or daughter will get further by obeying their parents than by just preaching at them. Most people move through three stages.

1. Their hearts become warm to Christianity;
2. Their minds become interested in it;
3. Their wills become obedient to Christ.

Stage one happens when they meet Christians, and find that a different sort of love unites the Christians, a love which builds a bridge of friendship into their own lives, over which Jesus can walk.

So the way we share Jesus with others is vital. Prepare leaders, or senior members, to do two role-plays (see Footnotes) of conversations about Jesus: in the first, a timid enquiry is met by a long, aggressive, sermon-like reply, full of jargon, and perhaps with the Christian prodding the enquirer fiercely in the chest with his finger! In the other, an aggressive questioner is answered by short, gracious, sensitive replies, which are unthreatened by the questioner's manner, and which gradually soften it. Ideally, this needs to be done very well, but there is still value if it isn't! Discuss the good and bad points in each conversation. You can either do the role-plays by everyone being involved, and therefore several small role-plays will all happen simultaneously, or by having one role-play, and observers. The latter enables greater control in preparation by the leaders; the former enables greater learning – although you, as a leader, are not then in as much control of what is being learnt!

Take action (10–15 mins)

Explain that it is those we love who will hear most clearly what we say to them about Jesus. Give a personal example, if appropriate. Get each person to complete base 4 from the 'Group Extra' sheet, and to mark with a cross those with whom God might want us to share Jesus.

Have a time of silent prayer for these people.

Distribute among the group a suitable selection of Gospel booklets (pay a visit to your local Christian bookshop, or ask the person in charge of your church bookstall). Allow time for them to be examined, and then discuss which they think is best, which is the least embarrassing to give to a friend and why, and how they might use one.

Invite group members to mention the names of people they would like to share Jesus with. Have a time of group prayer for the people. If you are going to play 'The Service Game' next time, ask members to bring appropriate items with them to next week's session. (See under 'Take a Break', in the following session).

Finish this week's session with a reference to the final session of this course next week on 'Serving God'.

Footnotes

Memory verse. Revise all previous verses (Romans 5:8, John 6:37, Luke 11:28 and Phillippians 4:6), and learn together Matthew

28:19–20 – 'Go, then, to all peoples everywhere and make them my disciples . . . And I will be with you always to the end of the age.' (by all means include the part omitted, if that doesn't make it too long for your group).

Leaders' summary. Everyone who knows Jesus has their own story of what happened, and what it means to them to be a Christian. We ought to be ready to tell our story when the opportunity arises. Jesus promises that he will be with us, helping us to say and do the things that will point people to him.

Music.

Be bold, be strong	LP11
Go forth and tell	LP 46 / MP 61 / SLW 96
How lovely on the mountains	LP 71 / M-79 / SF1 41 (176)
I'm not ashamed	MP 100
Make me a channel!	LP 124 / MP 153 / FS 97
Tell out my soul	LP 197 / MP 215 / HF 90 (498)

Roleplay. Role-plays are particularly good discussion-starters. They don't require dramatic ability, only a little imagination. They enable the participants to 'get under the skin' or to 'step into the shoes' of other individuals.

Here are some tips:

- They always need preparing well. It's often worth writing out a very brief description of each character to give to the participant. The more real to life they are, the better.
- The first time you use one, choose the more confident people.
- Always stop a role-play when it's going well; don't wait for it to run out of steam.
- Be sure to 'role up' before you start, and to 'de-role' once you've finished the role play. ie. as you ~~being~~ begin, get the players to say their assumed names, and, when you've finished, get them to say their real names at least twice, going round the circle of participants.
- Do a proper de-brief, to help them to express their feelings about the role-play, and also to draw out the lessons learned from it.

GROUP · EXTRA

BASE 2.

FINAL APPEARANCE Read Luke 24: 36–53.

Before He left the disciples, Jesus had to convince them of two things. First, in verses 39-43, He showed them that he was ...... second, in verses 44-47, He showed them. From the Bible, what now people's sins could be ...... The disciples were ...... of these things (verse 48), which means that they knew then, and could tell others about them. How do you think the disciples felt when Jesus told them this? (underline one or more).

Overwhelmed with excitement and bored
Quite indifferent
Terrified out of their wits
Alarmed but enthusiastic
Totally confused
Deeply despairing

Can we be witnesses of the same things? How? Look at verse 49. What would Jesus send down that the Father has promised? ...... (You can check by looking at Luke 11:13 or 12:12.)
How do you feel about being a witness? Mark with a cross where you think you are on this line.

NO WAY!   HELP!   PERHAPS, SOMEDAY!   OK, BUT!   HOORAY!

• Put another cross where you could be in 6 months time

BASE 5.

ALL THE ANSWERS

How would you answer if someone asked you...

Why do you believe in God?

What do you get out of Church?

How did you become a Christian?

Why do you read the Bible?

3

Truth, the whole truth and . . .
The content of a teaching evening

It's been an awful week for Chris, the youth leader. There have been big problems at work, his car broke down, the trains to work have been haywire, and he broke up with his girlfriend.

And now he is yet again late back from work. The youth group starts in thirty-four minutes, he has done precisely no preparation, and he is beginning to sweat.

In desperation, Chris looks up a quiet-time passage from two weeks ago. He remembers being struck by the account of Stephen before the Sanhedrin in Acts 6:15. Stephen had 'the face of an angel' 'Pretty apt for me right now – I could do with the face of an angel', he mutters, and jots down a few thoughts as he stirs the baked beans.

That evening, his group learn to be angel-faced in all sorts of difficult situations, and at 10.30 Chris slumps into his armchair with a yogurt, wondering how much skin his teeth have left.

We live very busy lives. Most of us can identify with Chris: there's never enough time to prepare our youth group teaching material as we know we should.

Chris thought he was teaching them God's word. But he wasn't.

This chapter is about that most important but neglected area of working out what the Bible is saying. It is the most important chapter in the book, so please don't leave it out! The next few pages will focus on how we understand the Bible text. The following chapter looks at how we apply it.

In preparing their material, many youth leaders are keen to focus on the presentation of their ideas, and often skip what they're trying to get across. They pay more attention to the gift wrapping than to the present. Know the feeling? It is called indigestion, and is caused by eating the pudding before the main course. It's tempting, but may well make you sick.

Know your subject

Teachers need to know and be excited by their subject. When I was at school we had a remarkable geography teacher whose knowledge and enthusiasm for his subject was so infectious that I ended up becoming a geography teacher too! We need to have an infectious, informed enthusiasm for our subject, the Bible, and for its subject, God.

They say, 'you can't teach what you don't understand'. And you cannot teach *simply* what you don't know deeply. So we need to have a clear grasp of our subject, before we can hope to teach it well to others.

> You can't teach what you don't understand. And you can't teach simply what you don't know deeply.

This all sounds horrendous! Am I really saying that we've got to know the Bible inside out before we can teach it? Well, no and yes.

No, of course we don't have to know all the Bible before we can begin teaching it. Who does? But if we are Bible teachers, we should be serious about the Bible – seeking to understand the broad span of what it is about. And yes, we do have to grasp the bit we are teaching before we can communicate it to our group. Again, 'you can't teach what you don't understand'.

Sadly, many leaders try to teach a Bible passage before they have understood it themselves. More serious than that, though, is when leaders think they have understood a passage when they haven't. They end up believing they are teaching people what the Bible is saying, when they're not.

What is the Bible?

The Bible is God's word, that is, God's reliable communication with people. It is God's word, written down. God speaks to people through his word.

But people are pretty deaf to God, hence the importance of teachers who will explain to people what God's word says. As we do so God speaks. That is incredibly powerful. It may not look it, but appearances deceive.

> God still speaks through what He has spoken (John Stott, *Understanding the Bible*, Scripture Union, 1972).

Now if we are telling people that God is saying something that he is not, then we put words into God's mouth which were never there in the first place. People can end up with all sorts of strange ideas about what God is like and what God is saying. So, to teach the Bible, we first have to understand it ourselves. This is an incredibly important task, though one we very often skimp on. It's so easy to be vague: 'Well, it's a passage on prayer, isn't it?', without asking exactly *what* it tells us about prayer.

When we are dealing with people and teaching the word of God, we must make sure it is the word of God we are teaching, and not just our own thoughts and ideas. Little wonder so many of our sermons and youth group evenings are boring – it is because we are not teaching what the Bible is saying. If we were, how could that possibly be boring?

Special One
Which Bible should I use?

The Bible was written originally in three languages.
- Hebrew for most of the Old Testament
- Greek for the New Testament
- Aramaic for half of Daniel and two passages in Ezra

Any Bible we use today is a translation from the original languages, based on copies of the original texts which themselves no longer exist.

The translator's task is to take the words from the original language and translate these into English, using words, idioms and grammar which we can understand. Our world is not the same as that of the Bible, so there are different ways of doing this.

- **The literal translation** keeps as close as possible to the original language, and so has quaint, difficult or clumsy English.
- **The free translation** carries ideas through to the English, but there is less concern with the exact words of the original. Free translations are sometimes called paraphrases.
- **The dynamic translation** translates words, idioms, grammar and the construction of the original language into their nearest possible equivalents in English. It still uses original words on historical and factual matters, but updates language, grammar and style.

Take, for example, Matthew 18:24

King James version (literal)	New International Version (dynamic)	Living Bible (free)
'And when He had begun to reckon, one was brought unto Him which owed Him ten thousand talents	'As he began the settlement, a man who owed him ten thousand talents was brought to him.'	'In the process, one of his debtors was brought in who owed him a million pounds.'

This means that in the range from literal to free, our modern translations may be placed as follows:

Literal		Dynamic		Free	
KJV		NIV		JBP	LB
NASB	RSV	NAB	GNB		
RV		NEB	JB		

KJV – King James'/Authorised Version
NASB – New American Standard Bible

RV – Revised Version
RSV – Revised Standard Version
NIV – New International Version
NAB – New American Bible
GNB – Good News Bible
JB – Jerusalem Bible
NEB – New English Bible
JBP – JB Phillips' translation
LB – Living Bible

For careful Bible study, a dynamic translation is probably the best to start with, complemented by one literal and, as a lower priority, one free translation.

Starting in the right place

The starting point is very important as it determines what we end up with. I would not dream of starting a recipe half-way through, but I'm a dab hand at starting half-way through when it comes to preparing for our youth group.

When we're trying to understand the Bible, we must start at the beginning. We must start with the Bible itself. For the moment, leave aside commentaries, Bible dictionaries and study aids, and concentrate on the text. If at all possible, read the whole Bible book from which the passage you are going to teach comes. Then read it again – or at least the chapters before and after the passage. Try to get an overall picture of what the writer was trying to say.

This sounds like drudgery, but there is no substitute for it. What is more, we may well find that the Bible comes alive for *us* as we see the whole flow of the Bible book rather than a few isolated verses.

Having read the book, or at least some of it, of which the passage is a part, now read the passage itself. Read it again, and the immediately surrounding verses, asking these questions:

- What is the writer trying to say?
- What is the main theme or idea running through this?
- Why does this verse/paragraph follow on from the one before it? And how does it follow on to the one after?

> Do your best to present yourself to God as one approved, a workman who does not need to be ashamed, but who correctly handles the word of truth (2 Timothy 2:15).

So read the text and be thoroughly familiar with it. Have a good idea of what it is saying. Think about it. Chew it over. Let it 'ferment' in your mind over a few days. Then go back to it and read it again. And as you are doing all this, make sure you are praying about it too. We are unable to understand the Bible rightly on our own, so we *must* ask for God's help.

There is no substitute for simply spending time with the Bible and becoming familiar with the passage, reading it prayerfully, and seeking to understand it for ourselves.

Only then should you turn for help.

Getting help

We are not alone in this. When we seek to understand the Bible there are three people to help us.

Yourself

You can help yourself by using your mind and by being disciplined. We've all got minds; this isn't just an exercise for academics. And we are called to use them when studying the Bible. In 2 Timothy 2:7 Paul urges Timothy to use his mind and rely on God to help him understand:

> Reflect on what I am saying, for the Lord will give you insight into all this.

There is a delightful balance here. Both hard work and dependence on God are essential to understanding the Bible.

The Church

The Church (that is, other Christians) can be a great help in understanding the Bible. They are a people we ignore at our peril. The Bible itself places great emphasis on the importance of teachers in the Church. We see this clearly in 1 and 2 Timothy and

Titus. The Church itself acts as a kind of sieve, a testing ground for different interpretations of the Bible.

Within the Church there are people of different backgrounds and abilities: those with razor sharp minds, those with theological insight and understanding, those with immense Bible knowledge, and those who think they can detect heresy a mile off . . . Some of these are in your church. Others (thankfully?) are not.

These days there are also many valuable commentaries and study aids. We would be wise to seek out those who have gifts which can help us in understanding the Bible.

So thank God for biblical theologians. Use the books they have written to help you understand the Bible. You may need to tread carefully here, but don't be an ostrich, missing the good by avoiding the bad. Ask your minister which books are useful, and which are best avoided.

The Holy Spirit

If the first two people are important, the third is indispensable. The Holy Spirit, the one through whom God's word was inspired, is also at hand for the Christian to help us understand it. He helps us as we use our minds to understand the text. But don't sit back, put brain in neutral and wait for the answers to fall from heaven. It is not like that. The Holy Spirit illumines our understanding as we use our minds.

It therefore makes sense that we should ask for the Holy Spirit's help. So, when we come to study the Bible, it is not just an empty ritual when we pray for understanding: we should pray very seriously, asking God to help us grasp his word.

'The best interpreter of any book is its author, because he alone knows what he intended to say.' John Stott, *Understanding the Bible*

Special Two

Tools for the job

The following are all helpful, and even necessary, for careful study of the Bible:

- **Bible.** For an explanation of different Bible translations, see Special One.
- **Concordance.** This lists all references in the Bible to a particular word, and is useful, for example, for doctrinal studies (see chapter 7). Make sure you get one which is a concordance for use with your version of the Bible – it makes life a lot easier. Some Bibles have a small concordance bound in at the back. These Bibles tend to be expensive, but it could be a good birthday present.
- **Bible Dictionary.** This lists in alphabetical order (like a dictionary, in fact!) references to the people and places mentioned in the Bible, and tells you about them. It may well be illustrated with photos and include maps.
- **Bible Introduction.** These books give short introductions to each Bible book, with information on, for example, the author, date and outline, of the contents. A good starter is Simon Jenkins' *The Bible from Scratch* (Lion Publishing).
- **Commentaries.** You can get these on the whole Bible, or on specific Bible books. They range from the incredibly detailed to the totally vague. I like the 'Bible Speaks Today' series from IVP, but ask your minister what he or she recommends.

Working on the passage

So, it's time to prepare the teaching session for next Sunday evening. You've got the passage, you've got the Bible book it comes from. You've got a resource to help you prepare. You feel familiar with the passage and its context, and you've prayed about it. You've got your mind in gear, you've chatted to some friends in your church about it, and you've got a commentary and a Bible dictionary to hand.

What now?

Don't forget you could make the Bible say almost anything. But if you're open and honest, and apply these 'six things to remember', you'll be on target.

1 Remember history: think 'them, then'

When you look at a Bible passage, ask these questions:

- Who wrote to whom?
- What were the circumstances?
- Why was it written?
- What would the original hearers have understood?

Consider an example passage from Leviticus:

> Say to them: 'Any Israelite or alien living among them who offers a burnt offering or sacrifice, and does not bring it to the entrance to the tent of meeting to sacrifice it to the Lord – that person must be cut off from his people' (Leviticus 17:8–9).

This seems puzzling for those of us who are not in the habit of making burnt offerings or sacrifices. But remember that it describes rules for making these burnt offerings before the whole system of offering sacrifices was superseded by the death of Christ.

Or again, think of Amos. We need to be aware when reading Amos that he is an 8th century BC prophet. He came from the south (Judah) but was preaching in the north (Israel, sometimes also called Ephraim). You can get all that from Amos 1:1 by using a simple commentary.

2 *Remember style: think 'poetry and prose'*

The Bible has been written in a number of different literary styles. So within the pages of Scripture, we find:

History (eg 1 & 2 Samuel)
2 Samuel 18:9: 'Now Absalom happened to meet David's men. He was riding his mule, and as the mule went under the thick branches of a large oak, Absalom's head got caught in the tree. He was left hanging in mid-air, while the mule he was riding kept on going.'

Prophecy (eg Isaiah, Jeremiah, Micah)
Jeremiah 17:5: 'This is what the Lord says: "Cursed is the one who trusts in man, who depends on the flesh for his strength, and whose heart turns away from the Lord."'

Gospel (eg Matthew, Mark)
Matthew 5:1–2: 'Now when he saw the crowds, he went up on the mountainside and sat down. His disciples came to him, and he began to teach them saying . . .'

Epistles (eg 1 & 2 Thessalonians, 1 & 2 Timothy)
1 Thessalonians 5:12: 'Now we ask you, brothers, to respect those who work hard among you, who are over you in the Lord and who admonish you.'

Apocalyptic (eg Daniel, Revelation)
Daniel 10:5–6: 'I looked up, and there before me was a man dressed in linen, with a belt of the finest gold round his waist. His body was like chrysalite, his face like lightning, his eyes like flaming torches, his arms and legs like the gleam of burnished bronze, and his voice like the sound of a multitude.'

Wisdom (eg Proverbs, Job)
Proverbs 6:6: 'Go to the ant, you sluggard; consider its ways and be wise!'

Poetry (eg Song of Solomon)
Song of Solomon 5:10–12: 'My lover is radiant and ruddy, outstanding among ten thousand. His head is purest gold; his hair is wavy, and black as a raven. His eyes are like doves by the water streams, washed in milk, mounted like jewels.'

It's pretty obvious, but today you don't understand a poem in the same way as you would a history book, and you wouldn't understand a gospel in the same way as you would a straight biography. That is because a gospel is selective and is written with a clear purpose and message in mind, whereas a biography is a more comprehensive account of an individual's life. So don't overlook the literary style of what you are reading.

Language is living, and changes over time. The words we use now can mean different things from what they meant a hundred years ago. And words we use mean different things from words other people use. What's a 'hood' in America and here? So bear in mind that language differs. One obvious example from the New Testament is that while we have one word for 'love' in English, the Greek of the New Testament period had four, each with a significantly different emphasis. This is where reference to a commentary can help us to understand the passage.

3 Remember context: think 'concentric circles'

We remembered history in order to understand what was going on when the passage was originally written. Remembering the context narrows the focus.

The most common single reason for failing to understand the Bible is that we fail to see the passage in its context. We fail to take into account the verses, or even chapters, surrounding the particular text we're looking at. For example, consider the parable of the Good Samaritan (Luke 10:30–37). 'In reply Jesus said: "A man was going down from Jerusalem to Jericho, when he fell into the hands of robbers. They stripped him of his clothes, beat him and went away, leaving him half-dead. A priest happened to be going down the same road, and when he saw the man, he passed by on the other side. So too, a Levite, when he came to the place and saw him, passed by on the other side. But a Samaritan, as he travelled, came where the man was; and when he saw him, he took pity on him. He went to him and bandaged his wounds, pouring on oil and wine. Then he put the man on his own donkey, brought him to an inn and took care of him. The next day he took out two silver coins and gave them to the innkeeper. 'Look after him,' he said, 'and when I return, I will reimburse you for any extra expense you may have.' Which of these three do you think was a neighbour to the man who fell into the hands of robbers?' The expert in the law replied, "The one who had mercy on him." Jesus told him, "Go and do likewise."'

Many people start at verse 30, and say that the message of the parable is an incentive and example for us to be nice to other people. It certainly is, but that is not really what the parable is about, as becomes a little more obvious when you read the immediate context (verses 25–29). Here an expert in the law asks Jesus, 'Teacher, what must I do to inherit eternal life?' (verse 25). There is a brief conversation, and then Jesus tells the parable. If you keep this context in mind, the parable of the Good Samaritan is about how someone can 'inherit' eternal life (verse 25). And Jesus is saying that you cannot earn eternal life, unless you behave like the Good Samaritan all the time – which none of us do.

Once we have considered the author's intention and the situation to which the passage was written, the styles of writing and the language, we need to remember that a text cannot mean to us what it could never have meant to the original readers. Consider another, for example, from Philippians 4:13: 'I can do everything through him who gives me strength' This verse has been used to encourage Christians in almost any endeavour, whereas Paul wrote it in the context of his mission to the Gentiles and God's enabling in this specific task. We have no right to immediately jump to the conclusion that, just because God strengthened Paul in his particular mission, he will always strengthen us at whatever task we are involved with.

It is helpful to think of the passage in terms of a set of concentric circles. We need to consider the passage's context in relation to all these circles, but the most important ones (and the ones where it is easiest to avoid making mistakes) are those nearer the middle.

Here are certain things to bear in mind which will keep us from dropping clangers.

- **Give-aways.** Look out for give-away words and phrases such as 'therefore', 'for this reason', 'and', 'and so'. These words or phrases form links with what went before, so you cannot hope to understand your passage or verse without looking at what went on before it. In the gospels, look for who Jesus is addressing. And in the parables look out for the last verse which is often a give-away.
- **What's the point?** Always ask the most important questions: What is the author trying to say? Why does he say it here, and in this particular way? Is there a common theme running through, and, if so, what is it?
- **Think 'chunks'** In order to understand the argument, think in terms of chunks of Scripture. These may well be paragraphs, but sometimes it is more helpful to group paragraphs together into larger chunks. This exercise is especially important in order to understand the epistles and gospels, but is also relevant elsewhere in Scripture. Again, ask of each chunk, 'What is the point?'

4 Remember simplicity: think 'understanding'

The Bible is God communicating with us. He communicates with us in order that we should understand what he is like, and live as he wants us to. God has spoken in the Bible in order to be understood. Therefore he wants it to be simple enough to understand.

But we can be terrible good at making even the most simple appear incredibly complicated! We take straightforward Bible passages and contort them to fit in with our own preconceived ideas, rather than taking them at face value.

Keep it simple, but don't be simplistic. Watch out for metaphors, parables and the like. Don't, for example, do a 'Nicodemus'. In John 3, Jesus explains to Nicodemus that he must be born again. Nicodemus took it literally, but Jesus meant it figuratively. We have to use common sense in understanding the Bible, especially when a literal understanding would produce bizarre consequences!

The English language uses different forms of speech:

- **Look out for similes** (eg 'dead as a door-nail', 'as white as freshly fallen snow') and metaphors (eg 'a glaring error', 'food for thought') and don't take them literally.
- **Keep an eye open for 'types'.** So, for example, Moses is a type of Christ in that he was a forerunner of Christ, and has certain characteristics repeated on a grander scale in Jesus. So the Passover in Exodus 12 is a forerunner of God passing over our sins because of the blood of Jesus.
- **Watch out for parables** where there tends to be one main point, eg the parable of the workers in the vineyard in Matthew 20
- **Spot allegories** where there is a more direct tie-in with reality at many points in the story, eg John 10:1-16. If in doubt, use a commentary to decide whether it is a parable or an allegory.
- **Watch out for figurative language,** and be very careful with it. Do not build a whole new doctrine on passages which are phrased figuratively, but pay special attention to the context of such passages. Look elsewhere in the Bible for support for what you think the passage is saying.

In short, don't be naive when studying the Bible, but keep it as simple and obvious as you can. That's generally how God intended it to be.

5 Remember purpose: think 'all one'

What is the Bible? What is it *for*? It is the main vehicle of God revealing himself to people so that we may be saved. And the main way God reveals himself to us is through Jesus Christ. The whole Bible points to Jesus. Remember this, especially as you read the Old Testament.

God reveals himself through the whole of the Bible, so do not ignore texts you disagree with or find difficult. It may well be precisely those we ignore that God wants to use to challenge us.

Instead let Scripture check your understanding of Scripture. This is because the Bible is a unity. It comes from one mind and speaks with one mind on all subjects it covers. It of course contains human variety and is written from different human viewpoints, hence the apparent differences. But if one bit seems to disagree

split inf.

with another, look more closely: a single divine Author does not contradict himself. Let Scripture interpret Scripture.

> The Bible is its own best interpreter . . . Unclear passages must always be interpreted by passages where the teaching on the same subject is clear, and not the other way round. (Brian Abshire, *Get More from your Bible*').

Within this, though, remember that truth can be many-sided. Different Bible passages may reveal different aspects of the same truth. For example, Christ is described in the Bible metaphorically as both a lion and a lamb. These do not contradict. Rather, they complement each other, as different facets of our understanding of Jesus Christ. In each case, the context points to the meaning.

Do not worry, though, if you cannot resolve and understand everything. The Bible talks of infinite things, and we've got finite minds, so we will never be able to understand it all. There will be passages we just haven't a clue about! With these.

- **Be relieved.** If we could understand everything about God, something would be seriously wrong.
- **Be honest.** Don't try to teach your group what you don't understand, as there can be nothing more damaging than this. If you don't understand something, say so, and your group will respect you for it.
- **Be humble.** Our world shouts at us that it is possible to understand and master everything, given time. There are parts of the Bible, though, that need eternity to grasp.
- **Be relaxed.** God will not reveal everything to us because we could not cope with it if he did. But God has revealed all we need in order to be saved and to serve him. So let's get on with it.

6 Remember authorship: think 'authority'

The Bible is an authoritative document because God is speaking.

The Bible must determine our response to the world around. Yet sadly, very often, the world around us determines what we think the Bible is saying. The Bible's message does not change, although the precise application of it does from time to time and from place to place, as our circumstances change.

If, therefore, you have some Christian experience (a dream, say), do not interpret the Bible in the light of your dream. Nor should you base your ideas on your dream, rather than on the Bible. Rather, interpret the dream in the light of what the Bible says on this matter. If a dream, vision, or 'word from the Lord' contradicts the Bible, this new information is not from God and should be rejected.

It is good to remind ourselves of this point: the Bible speaks to us authoritatively. We seek to understand it for a purpose. We are not involved in a dry, dusty academic exercise, but rather we want to understand the Bible so that we may know God better and obey him more.

And we want to teach it truthfully to our groups, so that they too may know God better and obey him more.

Seven Common Bungles

1 **Blindness,** where, for some reason, we just completely fail to see certain words which are blindingly obvious.
2 **Lack of time,** skipping the bits we think are unimportant – like, for instance, reading the surrounding verses – because we are preparing at the last minute.
3 **Arrogance,** where I think I already know what this passage is about, and impose my ideas on the Bible, rather than letting the Bible teach me.
4 **Hidden agendas,** where we know what we want to teach the young people, and we try and make the Bible say it. The result is ill-informed young people and imbalanced young Christians.
5 **Narrowness,** where the context is ignored. This is the most common mistake.
6 **Selectivity,** where we only teach our favourite parts of the Bible, and ignore the bits we dislike or disagree with.
7 **False applications,** where we apply the Bible before we have understood it.

Key Example One
Mark 1:1–15 – preparations

INTRODUCTION

This material is based on *Mark – Now Teach the Gospel* (CPAS, 1990). Please read these notes before using this with your group.

MARK 1

The beginning of Mark's gospel seems to be a hotchpotch of different ideas, thrown loosely together, to get the gospel off to a fast-moving start. But if you ask questions such as, 'What's the point?', 'What is Mark trying to say?', 'Is there a common theme running through this?' you begin to see that the theme of 'preparation' is dominant:

- Mark prepares the way for Jesus (1:1)
- The prophets prepare the way for Jesus (1:2–3)
- John the Baptist prepares the way for Jesus (1:4–8)
- God the Father prepares the way for Jesus (1:9–13)

All this lays the groundwork for Jesus' 'manifesto' in 1:14–15.

This theme of 'preparation' then is reflected in the 'Aim to Teach', which is that 'different people prepared the way for Jesus Christ', which is a summary of what the passage is saying, and the one thing that we want our young people to remember.

Make one point in one sentence: Different people prepared the way for Jesus Christ.

MARK 2

This looks at Jesus' 'manifesto' of Mark 1:14–15. The idea of a manifesto is something which young people can relate to, and is carried through to an exercise on the Group Extra sheet. You may not expect your young people to take these sheets home with them, but there is certainly educational value in filling in one of these sheets, if not at every session, then at least on a regular basis.

Take it in

This uses group discussion directed by the leader, who needs to make sure that the points mentioned are brought out in the discussion. She can point these out as things to note during the discussion.

Take Action

Preparations for Jesus and this study in Mark form concrete things which young people can do in response to this teaching evening.

Memory Verse

Learning Bible verses may have gone out of fashion, but is still most valuable for people of all ages, and it can be great fun if led well.

THE SESSION

Aim to teach that different people all prepare the way for Jesus Christ.

Aim that the group should

understand the outline of the Gospel, and prepare themselves for this study of Mark.

Leading this session

Before you start planning this first group session there are three things to check:
- Have you run the leaders' course (pages 4–10)?
- Have you read through Mark yourself (pages 11–12)?
- Have you read how to use these sessions (pages 13–14)?

If you couldn't say yes three times, please consider waiting until you can!

Warm up

You may want to use one of the following ice-breakers, especially if some of your group are new to each other or to the idea of studying the Bible together (see Leaders' Hints on ice-breakers).

    (a) Get your group to sit in a circle, facing inwards, and give them a tennis ball. They are to call out someone's name, and throw the ball to them. The person who catches the ball does likewise, but can only throw the ball to someone whose name they know. Carry on until the group knows all the names. Vary the pace. Do it to music, perhaps.

(b) Just to get people relaxed, try 'Are you sitting comfortably?' The group stands in a tight circle, facing the person in front of them, and then, all sit down gently on the knees of the person behind them. Congratulations if this actually succeeds, and, if it does, try to get them to walk backwards, slowly, in unison.

Introduce this session

Explain that

> Mark's Gospel is in two overlapping halves. The first half is from 1:1–9:7, and in this Mark tackles the question 'Who is Jesus?'. The second half starts around 8:27 and goes on to 16:8, and looks at the question 'What did Jesus come to do?' Or to put it more simply: part one – Who is this? part two – And what is He up to?

Ask the group, in pairs perhaps, to complete the 'Jesus Profile' on their GROUP EXTRA sheet (page 74 – have you done sufficient photocopies?) by ticking those they think are correct descriptions of Him. See if everyone agrees.

Explain that

> all that was just preparation, to get the minds working. In this evening's session we are looking at the preparations for Jesus' coming.

Read Mark 1:1–13

Possibly in four parts – Narrator, Isaiah, John the Baptist, Voice from heaven (have you thought of using Gospel Booklets? see Leader's Hints). Now split the group up into pairs and, for five minutes, get them to look at the passage and answer the question 'What is the common thread here?'

The thread which links this passage together is 'preparation'. Why?

Discuss the answers and then give an overview of the passage, which should include the following. If you can introduce the parts of this overview while you are discussing the answers, so much the better.

Mark prepares the way for Jesus (1:1). *This is his introduction to this passage, to his whole Gospel, and to the Person of Jesus. In it Mark introduces Jesus as the Son of God, which he spends the rest of the first eight chapters proving.*

The prophets prepare the way for Jesus (1:2–3). *Isaiah writes here about Jesus, hundreds of years before He was born and, in doing so, prepares the way for Him. The Old Testament only makes sense when interpreted in the light of the New Testament, and when we realise that it is pointing to Jesus Christ.*

John the Baptist prepared the way for Jesus (1:4–8). *Despite his popularity, John the Baptist points away from himself and towards Jesus. He is telling the people that the preparation they must make for Jesus is to repent and be baptised. In other words, they must have a change of mind, leading to a change of action, and there should be an outward sign of this inward change.*

God prepares the way for Jesus (1:9–13). *God the Father and God the Spirit prepare Jesus for what is ahead. God identifies with Jesus in Jesus' baptism, and Jesus identifies with mankind in His temptation. God, one with Jesus, one with us.*

Jesus completes His preparation by going into Galilee and beginning to preach. 1:14–15 is Jesus' manifesto. The preparations are now complete, the campaign begins. There is more teaching on this element in 'Mark 2'.

Take it in

Spend a little time concentrating on John the Baptist and his preparing the way for Jesus, especially on John pointing away from himself and to Jesus. End up with locust and wild honey sandwiches. (Use your imagination!)

Take a break

Can anyone do an impersonation of the Prime Minister, or other leading politician? Give them their chance now! Ask the group if they can remember the main points of the government's manifesto at the last election. Ask your impressionist to give an election speech. Provide drinks at this point if you plan to have them.

Read Mark 1:14–15

Ask what are the main points of Jesus' manifesto? Get them to complete (perhaps in pairs) the manifesto on the GROUP EXTRA sheet.

Take it in

As you discuss the answers, stress the three main points:

1. The time has come
All the prophets and John the Baptist were saying that the time had not yet come. Jesus arrives and says the time has come. In other words, He is pointing to Himself, and He is saying that now is the time for the Gospel. This brings in a sense of urgency.

2. Kingdom of God is near
This is the heart of Jesus' message. The heart of the Gospel is the breaking in of God's kingly rule. The Kingdom of God is where God, the King rules ie in the lives of those who follow Him, and 100% in Heaven. The Gospel is therefore, the rule of God in our lives, and Jesus is the content of the Gospel, as He not only illustrates it, but came to introduce it.

3. Repent and Believe
The Gospel is not only the objective fact of Jesus Christ, but what needs to be done, ie the hearers have to repent (change your mind, leading to a change of action) and also believe in the Good News (I believe that Jesus is King, and therefore live under His authority).

This is expanded later on in Mark. Mark is good news because, in his book, he explains the good news of God's kingly rule in Jesus.

Take action

All these preparations for Jesus' coming need to be applied personally, and possibly also at a corporate level within your group or church.

Ask the group to answer the following three questions, which are also on the Group Extra sheet, confidentially:–

1. How can I prepare for Jesus in my life?
2. How can I prepare for this study in Mark?
3. How can our group prepare for studying Mark's Gospel?

Pray quietly for two minutes about what the members have written. For next week, get your members to bring (in secret, so no one else knows) two personal items from their bedroom.

Memory verse

Mark 1:14–15: 'After John was put in prison, Jesus went into Galilee, proclaiming the good news of God. "The time has come", He said. "The Kingdom of God is near. Repent and believe the good news!"'

Equipment needed

- Photocopies of GROUP EXTRA (page 74)
- A ball
- Pens
- Mark's Gospels or Bibles

Music suggestions

Make Way, Make Way   CFW 587 LP 125
My Lord He is a-coming soon   CFW 588 LP 138
Prepare the Way   SHF 458
The Spirit of the Lord   LP 205

Commentary notes

1. Mark 1:1: Mark introduces Jesus as the Son of God, and records God the Father's acclamation of Jesus as His Son in 1:11. See also 9:7 and 15:39.

GROUP EXTRA

MARK 1:1-15

JESUS PROFILE

- ☐ Preacher
- ☐ Baptiser
- ☐ Fisher
- ☐ Sent from God
- ☐ Jew
- ☐ Powerful
- ☐ Shy

THE GOSPEL PARTY

Proclaiming the Good News

Galilee, Nazareth Ward

John the Baptiser introduces
JESUS OF NAZARETH:

Make your decision -
a change for the better, for ever.
"After me comes one who is greater than I am."
Jesus' Good News Manifesto:

1. _____
2. _____
3. _____

Eloi, Eloi, lama sab

1. How can I prepare for Jesus in my life?

THINK:
"God had only one Son, and He made Him a preacher."

2. How can I prepare for this study in Mark?

3. How can our group prepare for studying Mark's Gospel?

2. Mark 1:14: Preaching is dangerous – John has just been imprisoned for this, but here Jesus goes into Galilee preaching.

3. 'Proclaim' is literally to announce in a loud voice.

4. Jesus is at the centre of the text, right the way through this section. Keep Him there.

Leader's hints

Ice-Breakers: Some groups don't like 'playing games'. If you are that sort, you'll probably ignore such childish things as ice-breakers. Please don't. They can be great fun. They can relax a group so that real learning is much more likely to happen. They can make an evening more memorable. Take the plunge and get over that initial reluctance (which is more often from the leaders, anyway!) and you'll never look back.

Gospel Books: Why not buy your group copies of Mark's Gospel for this course? The Bible Society publish colourful and very well presented NIV's of Mark's Gospel, called 'The Power of God', or Good News Bible booklets called 'God in Action'. They should be available from your local Christian Bookshop sold in tens at a reduced rate.

Key Example Two

Mark 8:31–38 – 'Christianity without Tears'

INTRODUCTION

This is based on *Mark – Now Teach the Gospel* (CPAS).

This material shows the importance of looking for a common theme which links different parts of the passage together. Please read these notes before using this example with your group.

Aim to Teach

In teaching Mark's gospel, it is essential to have a firm grasp of it first. This means reading it all, preferably more than once. Mark is a fascinating story and is not that long – an hour is plenty of time to leave for a quick initial read, and a fast reader would get through Mark twice in this time. If you can, though, take a more leisurely stroll through Mark. The key to understanding the general spread of Mark is to see that it is in two overlapping halves. The first half (1:1–9:7) looks at the question 'Who is Jesus?' The second half (8:31–16:8) concentrates more on 'What did Jesus come to do?'

Without an overall understanding of Mark's gospel, Mark 8:31–38 is very difficult to teach well.

Mark 8:31–38 is the beginning of the second half of Mark – ie Mark has established who Jesus is, and now he is beginning to look at why Jesus came. Hence the 'aim to teach', which reflects both of these: 'Jesus – the King who came to die'.

Read Mark 8:31–33

Note, too, this view of the overall structure of Mark can be shown to the group. It is not a mystery just for leaders, but will help everyone understand Mark more clearly. This is not just an academic exercise: it applies directly to life now, as we learn that the Christian life is one of service and suffering.

Take it in

This helps to clarify what group members think about who Jesus was. This is a good way of initiating thinking about someone's identity.

Take a break

This is a bit of fun, but still firmly linked into the passage.

Read Mark 8:34–38

Again, this helps understanding of the passage, and comes from an understanding of the overall thrust of Mark's gospel.

THE SESSION
Aim to teach

that Jesus, the King, came to die.

Aim that the group should

begin to grasp the idea that following Jesus involves following His example of sacrifice and service.

Leading this session

This session is the backcloth for the rest of the Gospel. It is the first time Jesus specifically links His Messiahship with His death.

   Be as practical as possible. The passage teaches first about the suffering Messiah and then applies that to the life of the disciple. Do the same, and, all the way through, help your group see how this applies to specific situations. Try to avoid letting them get away with vague generalities

Warm-up

Ask your group members to do the crossword in the GROUP EXTRA page. All the answers to the across clues are in this passage (either NIV or GNB), and many of the down clues also relate to Mark. You could split the group into pairs or threes and have a competition to see who finishes first.

The answers are:

Across	Down	
1. SON OF MAN	1. SOB	10. DEAF
6. GOD	2. NAG	11. EAT
8. BEGAN TO	3. FUNGICIDE	12. PRE
10. DISCIPLES	4. AGO	13. SIT
12. PRIESTS	5. NO	14. SAD
15. FOR	7. DAYS	16. OR
17. REJECTED	9. ELI	

Introduce this session

by reviewing what you taught (and what the group learned) when looking at Mark 8:11–30. You may like to ask them to write down five 'memory-jogger' words from the last session, and give them fifteen seconds to do this, then brainstorm them, and ask them to explain their contributions. You could remind them of the identikit pictures, if they are still around; or of the composite 'Jesus Profile' sheets. Mark's picture of Jesus is now coming together.

Explain that this passage is very closely linked to the previous one. Last time we saw Peter understanding that Jesus is the Christ. This week reveals that he still doesn't understand what sort of Christ Jesus is (a suffering-Christ). And we also learn that, since Jesus is a suffering-Christ, being His disciple means following His way of serving and suffering too.

Read Mark 8:31–33

You will need to explain the overall structure of Mark's Gospel, and show how this section is at the beginning of Part 2, which examines and answers the question "What did Jesus come to do?". You may like to ask your group what it new about v31, and what is old about it. Why is verse 31 so chilling?

Make it clear that in the last session Peter at last began to grasp who Jesus was, and that now Jesus goes on immediately to talk of His death. This would have been very hard for the disciples to grasp (hence Peter's reaction, v32). If Jesus is the Messiah, how can He die? If sovereignty lies ahead, why is He predicting suffering? How can Jesus reign eternally, and die? Isn't this a great contradiction? You may like to leave this hanging in the air, and take it up again in the second reeading from Mark.

Take it in

Play 'Who am I?' – a variation on the method of last time. Have two or three small teams (perhaps with some spectators, if you have a large group) and then give them clues, one at a time, to the identity of various people. Award ten points to any team which guesses right after one clue, eight points if they get it right after two clues, five points after three, three points after four, and one point after five. You may like to think up your own characters, perhaps including local celebrities (the vicar!) Here are two examples (check the details are still correct):

1. Lady Thatcher

(a) I was educated at Somerville College, Oxford..
(b) I am, by training, a chemist.
(c) I own a private house in London.
(d) My father was a grocer in Grantham.
(e) I am the Conservative MP for Finchley.

2. Billy Graham

(a) I was born in 1918
(b) I live in North Carolina.
(c) My wife is called Ruth.
(d) I am a preacher, known to many by a catchphrase "The Bible says ..."
(e) I spoke at Mission England in 1984 and Mission '89.

When you've finished this game, say that we might know who they are, but very few of us know what being them entails. (For example, Mrs Thatcher sleeps for four hours a night, and works seven days a week, etc.) More than that, we don't really understand what being a follower of them involves, eg being on the Cabinet ... There are parallels here with Peter, in that he didn't know what being the Messiah entailed, or what being a follower of His involved.

Ask then, why the group thinks Jesus spoke sternly to Peter in v33. Accept any suggestions, and try to draw out the very real temptation Jesus faced of avoiding the cross. Not to suffer for us in obedience to God would make His whole life meaningless. It was the centre of everything. His suffering for us is crucial (and so is *our* suffering – see the second reading from Mark).

Take a break

You may like to try the GGR (Greater Galilee Radio) Interview. Ask your group to put themselves into Peter's position. They are about to be interviewed on GGR. Ask a few to be interviewers, and to think of two important questions. Ask the rest to think carefully about what Peter was thinking about at the time, who he thought Jesus was, and how this was going to affect him, etc. (You will have to prime your interviewers quite carefully.) Then conduct the interviews, perhaps with you being the continuity announcer.

Read Mark 8:34–38

Peter and the disciples have failed to understand the nature of Jesus' Messiahship. The Messiah (anointed, designated one) came as a servant, to suffer and die for the sin of His people. He is a suffering-servant-saviour. And those who follow Him, must follow this example too, and serve sacrificially. We often say that we want to be 'like Jesus'. If you mean such a prayer, it will mean a life of suffering and rejection, losing your life, but gaining the one thing which is worth having in this world.

Teach your group that taking up one's cross involves denying yourself (v34), losing your life for Christ's sake and the gospel's (and thus saving it, v35), losing the world (and gaining life, v36), and being unashamed of Christ and His words (v38).

Take it in

Ask your group to fill in the "Cross-Carrying" table on the GROUP EXTRA sheet. First they should score themselves honestly for each of the four actions. Then they should decide on, and write down areas of action for each of the other three columns. It will work best if you give them some real personal examples to start them off (See *Leaders Hints*). Make sure you and they are specific in what you say.

Take action

Ask your group members to decide on *one* thing they're going to do in the next 24 hours, in order to put into practice something which they have learned tonight. Encourage them to write it privately in the "24 Hour Action" box on GROUP EXTRA. Then pray quietly about this course of action which needs to be taken.

Memory verse –

Mark 8:34

Music suggestions

From Heaven you came	LP 40 CFW 449
In the tomb so cold	LP132 MW 1
Meekness and majesty	LP 138
The price is paid	LP206 SHF 528
Take up your cross	HTC 114

Commentary notes

v31: Son of Man – Jesus alone uses this phrase, and describes Himself in this way 84 times in the New Testament (14 times in Mark). Jesus used this title for a number of reasons: to identify with us; to show that the 'Messiah', as they understood the term, was an inadequate title; because it carried with it the idea of suffering; because of the significance of the reference to it in Daniel 7:13, and Jesus would want to hint at this in His introduction of 'the last days'.

This is one of three times in Mark when Jesus foretells His death and resurrection. The other two (more detailed prophecies) are in 9:31 and 10:33–34.

v33: Jesus' strongest temptation was to avoid the cross, hence the sternness of His rebuke of Peter.

v34: To take up one's cross signifies a death march, publicly carrying your own death warrant.

v35: If life is what you hang onto, you end up with nothing. If life is not that important to you, you gain real life.

v38: This is the first clear reference to the Second Coming in Mark.

Leader's hints

Example. When you are asking the group to share something personal with each other, or as in this session to fill in a table privately with honest answers about their personal growth, your own example in setting the tone is crucial. If you are able first to give a personal example which is real, they are more likely to do the same afterwards. If you are able to show yourself as weak, as a failing Christian; then they will find it easier to be honest too. If you can't do this then you must question whether the Bible passage has really spoken to you yet, and if you ought to be teaching it to others.

GROUP EXTRA

THINK:
Just as Jesus was tempted to avoid the cross so we, His followers, are tempted to opt for a Christianity without tears. The devil will always try to get us to duck weakness, suffering, pain in our Christian life. But if we are truly to follow Jesus we must speak as sternly to Satan as He did, and also learn to shoulder the cross.

24 HOUR ACTION

CROSSWORD

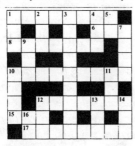

All the "Across" answers are found in Mark 8:31-38 (NIV or GNB)

Clues Across

1. Jesus (3,2,3)
6. Deity (3)
8. ___ ___ teach (5,2)
10. Clips side (9)
12. Clergy (7)
15. Since (3)
17. Jet creed (8)

Clues Down

1. Weep (3)
2. Scold (3)
3. Wipes out mushrooms, for example (9)
4. Past hidden in a Gospel (3)
5. "we have __ bread" Mk. 8 (2)
7. "..killed, and after three ___" Mk. 8 (4)
9. High Priest (3)
10. Condition of man in Decapolis - Mk. 7 (4)
11. "dogs under the table ___" Mk. 7 (3)
12. "four thousand men were ___sent" Mk. 8 (3)
13. "told the crowd to ___" Mk. 8 (3)
14. Young man left like this in Mk. 10 (3)
16. Gold alternative (2)

CROSS-CARRYING

	ACTION to do NOW	How am I doing? (marks out of 10)	Areas where I could easily progress	Tougher areas (long term aims)
a) Denying myself				
b) Losing my life for Christ's sake and the gospel's				
c) Losing the world				
d) Unashamed of Christ and His words				

4

'You Mean Me?' –
Helping young people apply the Bible

Christ Church have been rethinking their youth work, and now it all takes place on a Friday evening. They have a social slot first, with games, loud music, low lights, and then at 9 o'clock the stressed youth leaders try and calm people down for the serious part of the evening.

It's not an easy job. Many young people leave, or try to, and those who remain are noisy, disruptive, and unwilling to learn anything at all. The three leaders do their best to entertain the crowd (they hesitate to call them a group), and to keep the programme relevant. This week, it's guidance. In her preparation, Sally, who is in overall charge, has noted down the areas the young people need to hear about, and thinks that Psalm 37 answers most of these points. Those that it doesn't, she can mention anyway.

When it comes to the meeting itself, Sally reckons that the way to keep it relevant is to keep their questions at the top of the agenda. So she dives in with the application, and picks out a series of 'blessed thoughts' which she thinks will help everyone learn about guidance.

It doesn't help, though. The group is just as disruptive and as uninterested as it usually is.

Have Sally and her fellow leaders done anything wrong? Or are we to expect that sort of reception? Is this a right way to handle the Bible?

'The essence of knowledge is, having it, to apply it.' – Confucius.

This chapter is about how to discover what Scripture has to say to us *today*. This is very important. There's very little point in reading the Bible as you might a Jeffrey Archer novel on holiday, or an academic text book in the college library. The Bible was never intended just to be read. In Matthew 7:24 Jesus talked about people *doing* what he said: 'Therefore, everyone who hears these words of mine and puts them into practice is like a wise man who built his house on the rock.' The primary way that God achieves change in our lives is through the work of the Spirit as we apply the Bible to our lives.

Sadly we are so often content with a slightly academic Bible study where we neither seek to see how the Bible can be applied, nor do we get round to applying it.

Owls, ostriches and lemmings

Many of the problems of application dissolve when we return to the text and see what was really said in the first place. Let's have a close look at Acts 4:32-37, as an example.

> '(v22) All the believers were one in heart and mind. No one claimed that any of his possessions was his own, but they shared everything they had. (v33) With great power, the apostles continued to testify to the resurrection of the Lord Jesus, and much grace was upon them all. (v34) There were no needy persons among them. For, from time to time, those who owned land or houses sold them, brought the money from the sales, (v35) and put it at the apostles' feet, and it was distributed to anyone as he had need. (verse 36) Joseph, a Levite from Cyprus, whom the apostles called Barnabas (which means Son of Encouragement, (v37) sold the field he owned and brought the money and put it at the apostles' feet.'

As with all application, there are three possible approaches to this passage: that of the ostrich, the lemming, or the owl.

- The ostrich says, 'Well, fine for them then, but it says nothing to us now.'
- The lemming says, 'If they did it, then so should we.'
- The owl says, 'Let's understand the text, and then think about applying it.'

Three things are clear about what the early church actually did.

1 **Their giving was sporadic.** Some versions do not translate a rather important word in the original, which the NIV readers in v34 as 'from time to time'. This selling of lands and houses was an occasional activity by some Christian believers. They did not all do it all at the same time, and neither is there evidence of a communal purse, topped up by the occasional deal on the property market.

sp.
? renders

2 **Their giving was voluntary.** They didn't have to, but rather they chose to do it because their attitude to their possessions changed radically after they became Christians. What they owned was no longer so important.

3 **Their giving was according to need.** Not everyone benefited directly, only the needy. They did not do it so that the communal lot could be improved.

These three facts alone should convince us that the passage is not a mandate to set up a Christian 'community' in which all possessions are shared.

But how should this be applied?

These were the actions of a Spirit-filled community (v31), and we need to learn from their change of attitude to their possessions, their generosity and their love. That *may* lead some of us to sell homes and lands, and give the money so that the church could help the needy. That would not be wrong. It would be very generous. But at the same time Acts 4 does not demand it.

Four rules for application

There are four straightforward rules you can use for application. Two are positive, and two are negative:

- Imply rather than apply
- Be general rather than specific
- Don't be legalistic
- Don't apply everything

Rule 1: *Imply rather than apply*

You are giving a talk. You have said what the passage means and now you want to apply it to the lives of your young people. You have been talking about prayer, and say that this means that young Christians should be setting aside ten minutes each day to pray.

Is this right?

I'm not sure we can be that specific. The precise application of the Bible will vary from person to person. You and I may both be convicted of our prayerlessness, but change our prayer lives as a result in totally different ways. And besides, we cannot possibly hope to know each individual in our groups well enough in order to make the right specific application every time. That is not the role of the youth leader anyway. To operate in that way veers dangerously towards dictatorship rather than Christian leadership. It also results in legalism, as we lay down laws for our young people to keep.

So, think in terms of implications. We explain the passage, and then say what the implications are for Christians today. Give specific examples of how this has applied to others. Drive home the necessity of application, but don't say 'this is what you must do because of this passage'.

Application is for the hearer. We spell out the implications, they make the applications.

Rule 2: *Be general rather than specific*

Some find it useful to divide applications into general and specific categories. The general refers to principles from the Bible to be followed by all people of all ages, for instance, 'Love your neighbour'. But, these are not a lot of use unless they are backed up by specific applications. Each person needs to ask, 'What should *I* do?'

Applications need to be personal (I need to change, not my neighbour), precise (include as much detail as you possibly can), and practical (so that it is actually achievable).

Leaving an application at a general level is like using a spray can when painting, when what is actually needed is a fine paintbrush and the attention to details that goes with it.

Three aims for application

- **Personal.** Give an example of how someone known to you had their attitudes to their possessions changed. Even better, use an example of someone known to the group. You could use yourself occasionally as an example, but don't overdo it.

- **Precise.** Say exactly what they did. Don't be vague and leave it at 'they no longer saw their house as their own'. What difference did that make? Be as specific as possible.

- **Practical.** What did this person you know actually *do?* Obeying the Bible often means taking practical action, and changing your lifestyle. So what practical difference has been made?

Rule 3: Don't be legalistic

The great danger with youth leaders applying the Bible to the lives of their members is that it all becomes legalistic.

Avoid teaching *the* Christian response. Rather, help your young people think through how they as Christians can respond to this personally and individually. Avoid setting up new laws which young people feel they have to keep. 'Christians have to read their Bibles for ten minutes every day', 'Christians have to go to church twice every Sunday.'

> Somehow we need to bring young people into that kind of contact with God's word that carries them beyond understanding it to the place where the divine perspective permeates personality, shapes values, and is expressed in decision (Lawrence O. Richards, *Youth Ministry: Its Renewal in the Local Church*).

Rule 4: Don't apply everything

Some people try to apply everything in the Bible. But not all the Bible is directly and easily applicable. Some is primarily for our instruction and edification. If you can't think of direct applications of, say, Isaiah 40:25–26, do not worry. Let the passage speak for itself as it offers a picture of the greatness of God:

'To whom will you compare me? Or who is my equal?' says the

Holy One. (v26) 'Lift your eyes and look to the heavens: who created all these? He who brings out the starry host one by one, and calls them each by name. Because of his great power and mighty strength, not one of them is missing.'

Guidelines for being an owl

Ostriches avoid the point and lemmings do not think. The key to being an owl is to think through what the text originally meant. Only when you believe you've grasped the intention of the author and the message the original readers or hearers would have understood, can you go on to link it with the 20th century.

The wise youth leader will take the following steps:

- HEAR what the text said to the orignal hearers.
- LOOK out for the original situation.
- THINK about the intention of the original writer.
- LINK with the 20th century by suggesting implications.

- **HEAR what the text said to the original hearers**
  Consider an example from Joshua 1:9

  'Have I not commanded you? Be strong and courageous. Do not be terrified; do not be discouraged, for the Lord your God will be with you wherever you go.'

The usual application of this is to find encouragement for any and all difficult situations in life today. But if you hear what it meant to Joshua, you have to think more deeply before you apply it. Joshua had just taken over the leadership of the people of Israel from Moses, and is about to start a military campaign to take the land which God had promised to the people of Israel. In that context, the verse is deeply meaningful to Joshua. The 'wherever you go' refers to wherever Joshua goes in the promised land.

This is not God's promise to solve our problems of agoraphobia, and nor can we apply it to other situations which we find threatening. This *does* teach us about God's care and concern for his people. That is as true today as it was then. But we cannot lift this verse straight out of the Old Testament, and tie it round our necks as we go for our next job interview, without first thinking a little more carefully about it.

- **LOOK out for the situation**

  In any Bible passage, try to discover the situation facing the readers or hearers. An important point is that for the New Testament our situation now is the same as for them, then. Along with the early church, we both live in the 'last days', and so there is a close parallel between our situation and theirs. For the Old Testament the situation is different. We now see the Old Testament as pointing forward to Jesus, and we need to read the Old Testament through the window of Jesus Christ.

  We can apply Romans 3:22–23 today because mankind's situation is just the same now as then, and God does not change.

  > There is no difference, for all have sinned and fall short of the glory of God.

  The rules for church leaders in 1 Timothy 3:1–7 still hold because we still have churches now with leaders who do a similar job.

  > Now the overseer must be above reproach, the husband of but one wife, temperate, self-controlled, respectable, hospitable, able to teach . . .

  But the law about priests in Leviticus 21:5 does not transfer across because we are no longer ethnically designated the people of God all together in one place: we are living under a new covenant rather than the old covenant, and our priests are not the same as their priests.

  > Priests must not shave their heads or shave off the edges of their beards, or cut their bodies.

- **THINK about the intention of the original writer**

  We must ask what the author *intended* to convey as he was writing. This has particular relevance for narratives (eg 1 and 2 Samuel, Acts), and is also relevant for other parts of the Bible.

  Most biblical material conveys information which is descriptive. It paints a picture and helps us to understand what is going on and what was being said. But it is not meant to give instructions for us to follow now. So, for example, when Naaman the leper is told by Elisha to 'wash yourself seven times in the Jordan, and your flesh will be restored, and you will be cleansed' (2 Kings 5:10), this is not a general cure for all who have leprosy. The writer of 2 Kings intended to convey other truths by this story, not least the need for humility.

Generally, unless the Bible tells us that we must do something, what is described in a narrative section can never be a command for us now. It may be a good example, or a bad one – and it's often up to us to decide which. But very rarely does the Bible use descriptive sections as direct commands for us now. This does not reduce their value, and indeed some of the richest parts of Scripture fall into this category.

Where the intention is not clear, you and your group may decide to copy a biblical pattern. For instance, you may decide to follow the example of Acts 13:3 by fasting and praying, and then placing hands on those who are going off abroad to work for a missionary society.

> So after they had fasted and prayed, they placed their hands on them and sent them off.

But you will respect other groups who don't want to and don't feel the need to do this.

- **LINK with the 20th century by suggesting implications**
  In order to help group members apply the Bible, there are three questions which you can ask of any passage. These questions will help you see if and how it could apply to your life, and therefore help you suggest the implications it has for your group members.

- *Is it moral?*
  Distinguish between matters which are inherently moral and those which are not. Those which are moral probably should be applied today. Those which are not are less easily applicable to the 20th century. God's standards of right and wrong remain the same, and are important relevant today. They may need some care over application, but the general rule is – where morals are concerned – look hard, and aim to apply them today.

  By the same token, there are many commands in the Bible which are not morally based. For example, there is the command to 'greet all the brothers with a holy kiss' in I Thessalonians 5:26. In this case, there is less reason for applying it directly today.

- *Is it consistent?*
  Draw a clear dividing line between where the Bible, and especially the New Testament, always takes a consistent line on an issue, and where it has contrasting views. Where the Bible has a variety of views, this probably reveals an issue where it would be foolish to be dogmatic. In teaching our groups, it would be wise to give both sides of the argument for a balanced biblical view, tell them what we believe, and get them to make up their own minds.

An example of the former is murder, where the Bible has a consistent view. It is against it.

On the other hand, when you look at forms of organising the ministry in the New Testament, there is a whole range of methods. Is there a consistent biblical model of a hierarchy of leadership in the form of bishops, priests and deacons? No, there is not. Is there a consistent name for Christian ministers, such as priests, presbyters, elders or ministers? No, there is not.

Here we would be foolish to apply one particular model and then say that everyone must follow it. Of course, you may wish to apply one biblical pattern to your own situation, but we should allow other people to be at liberty to do other things if they wish.

● *Is there a principle?*
There is a difference between where the Bible is laying down a principle, and where it is applying one and therefore giving an example. If you have a passage where a principle is being set out, then take careful note.

So, for example, Paul sets out the principle of living sacrifices in Romans 12:1.

> Therefore, I urge you brothers, in view of God's mercy, to offer your bodies as living sacrifices, holy and pleasing to God – this is your spiritual act of worship.

We should carefully seek to apply this to ourselves, and to show our groups the implications it has for them. On the other hand, Paul's personal testimony at the end of his life in 2 Timothy 4:7 is an example of Paul applying this same principle to his own life. But we should be careful before jumping straight to applications today from this particular example.

> I have fought the fight, I have finished the race, I have kept the faith.

Principles are easier to apply than examples.

What about the Old Testament?

There is no doubt that most people find the New Testament easier to understand and teach than the Old. To be honest, there are more difficulties in understanding the Old Testament, and particular difficulties when applying it. So what shall we do with all those Old Testament laws, and the violence, and the long lists of people?

Here are a few suggestions to help us through.

- Look to learn about Jesus from the Old Testament. The Old Testament is about Jesus. In fact, look at the Old Testament through the New Testament.

- Respect the Old Testament laws. They remain God's word, even though for us they are no longer God's commands. They formed the basis of God's relationship with his people Israel, and are the backbone of the Old Testament which is essential for our understanding of the New. They still reveal God's character. But only in Christ do we see God's character completely.

- Work out which of the Old Testament laws the New Testament supports and restates, and which it updates and supersedes. If the New Testament supports and restates, it is a law for today, to be applied by us and our groups. This, for example, includes the ten commandments.

- Look beyond the details of specific laws for the reasons they were important in Old Testament days. You will discover the underlying principles of which the law was but an application. So, for example, Deuteronomy 24:18 gives the reason for the law in Deuteronomy 24:17.

  > Do not deprive the alien or the fatherless of justice, or take the cloak of the widow as a pledge. (v17)

  > Remember that you were slaves in Egypt and that the Lord your God redeemed you from there. That is why I command you to do this. (v18)

- Remember that Old Testament narratives are primarily examples and illustrations. They are not automatically (because they are in the Bible) examples of good and right behaviour. Sometimes they highlight bad behaviour, and it is up to us to notice that.

Special One
Application and your group

Here is the nitty gritty. You have applied the passage to yourself, personally. You have thought how it may apply to your young people. Now you need to give them every opportunity to apply God's word for themselves and therefore take action. How is this best done? Here are a few suggestions:

- **Be specific.** Vague application results in little action, and more probably no action at all. Instead, ask how your young people are going to apply what they have learned today.

- **Be memorable.** Try and make your teaching memorable. Back it up by getting them learning things, even by rote, because what your young people remember they are more likely to apply.

- **Be bold.** (But be careful not to domineer.) Sometimes, ask your young people to tell a friend what they are going to do in order to apply what they have learned. Of course, this assumes that they have learned something and that they do want to apply it, and that they have a friend to give them a let out. Or get them to write down what they will do, or talk together about possible applications. We need to help each other to obey God.

- **Be prayerful.** Pray about your own application of the passage, and pray that your group would apply it too. Pray that the spiritual battle of putting our faith into practice would be won.

- **Be challenging.** Give a time limit. People who know about these things suggest that unless we have taken at least some action towards implementing good resolutions within 36 hours, we never will.

- **Be patient.** Remember God usually works in us and changes us gradually. Lots of small steps result in certain and significant progress. Impress this on your group and do not expect vast leaps forward.

- **Be sensitive.** People do fail. They do get downhearted. We constantly fail to apply God's word. Be encouraging at all times and sensitive to people's feelings, frustrations and failures.

- **Be consistent.** We may determine to do something and then forget to put it in to practice. Ask the group members – and yourself – the following week how you got on. This could be done in an up-front manner, during personal chats, or through small group work.

Extra Time

Reading, understanding and applying the Bible is not difficult. We can all do it. In this chapter we have thought more deeply about it, but in essence the Bible speaks clearly to us now. It is simple and straightforward so that we can all understand it.

Of course the Bible is also profound. We can all get out of our depth. But we can also paddle quite safely, and gradually learn to swim.

God speaks in order to be understood by everyone. As we read our Bibles, and teach our young people, the Holy Spirit will get the message through to us and to our young people – despite all our frailties and fallibilities.

Much Christian youth work is invisible. And much of the work you put in is invisible too. Very few people will notice your hours of preparation as you seek to understand the passage and sort out the implications for your young people.

Very few will appreciate the time you spend working on presentation ideas.

Very few will say 'thank you'.

But all this invisible work reaps rewards. Young people understand the Bible. They begin to apply it to their lives and read it rightly themselves.

There is a lot of hard work behind that, but it's well worth it.

Key Example One

Ephesians 2:1–10: Saved – By God

INTRODUCTION

Please don't use this example now. Read the following few notes first!

Briefing

The key to applying the Bible rightly is to understand it rightly, and so the work which has gone on behind Briefing, First Half and Second Half, may be unseen but it's crucial. The analysis of the passage and simple but true understanding of it are vital.

This also feeds into the rest of the session.

Warm-up

All three ideas are based on good news and bad news which is the theme underlying Ephesians 2. They introduce the idea in a fun way while breaking the ice.

First half

Leadership needs sensitivity, so the Guess Who? game could go too far unless the leader has this quality. People who are upset often won't learn what we want them to, so be careful about games, or other comments or activities like this which may cause concern or upset in a group evening.

Half-time

As youth leadership involves the leaders sharing themselves with their youth group, the opportunity of giving a testimony may be useful. But don't overdo it and always give examples from your past history. Our job is to teach the Bible, not to teach our young people about us.

Second half

Again this is concentrating on the passage so that it can be applied correctly by individuals. There is a mixture of ideas here, but note the importance of *words*. There are elements of explanation and a brief talk on *why* God has acted in this way. Even in the silent 'right and wrong' game, the words at the end are most important, as they verbalize and summarize the non-spoken communication that has happened during the activity.

Final whistle

Applications must flow naturally from correct understanding of the text. At this stage our young people should be one step ahead of us, already applying the Bible to their lives because they have understood it. We can give possible examples, but we musn't lay down rules of what *must* be done because of this passage.

The use of small groups to work out application helps young people to be specific, and is more likely to produce changed lives as we encourage each other to action.

THE SESSION

Teaching point

We have been saved from our sin by God's action, not ours.

Group action

Aim that your group members would genuinely thank God for what he has done in their lives.

Briefing

This passage is in two distinct sections. Verses 1–3 talk about our state before we became Christians (and the state of non-Christians now). Verses 4–10 talk about what God has done to save us.

It is probably best to look at the first three verses and then verses 4–10, so that First half covers verses 1–3 and Second half covers verses 4–10.

Warm-up

Try one of these:

Find that Story. Divide your group into two or more teams (teams should have no more than six members), and give each team one copy of the same day's newspaper. For example, each team might have a copy of Tuesday's *Daily Mail*. Use questions which you have prepared beforehand, the answers to which are found in the paper. Have a short competition, with members coming to you with their answers.

Adverts. Divide up into teams and give each team several old newspapers and ask them to sift through their papers and come up with a slogan or advertising feature for your group, based on the headlines. Cut these out and stick them to another sheet of paper to form a decorative collage.

Thread a Needle. After any of the above newspaper games, ask your group members to thread themselves through one sheet of newspaper by tearing a hole in it and slipping through. With ingenuity even the largest can get through a tabloid!

Kick-off

Introduce the session by saying that newspapers are about news, and that is what this evening is about: bad news and good news. There is bad news about mankind and very good news about God.

First half

Guess who? Give each of your group members one record card and a pen. Ask them to think of a non-Christian friend who they know well and who is also known by some other members of your group. Tell them to write their friend's name on one side of the record card. Ask them then to write down a detailed description of their friend on the other side, but without mentioning their name on this side of the card.

Now they can either swop cards with other group members, and ask them to guess the names, do it all together as one group, or split into small groups and do the 'guess who' with the others in the smaller groups.

What you do now depends on how subtle you want to be. You could say that this is our view of non-Christians, but let us see what God's view is. You read out Ephesians 2:1–3. Alternatively, explain that we view people from the outside, but we also need to see ourselves and our friends from the inside. Again, read Ephesians 2:1–3. Finally, you could explain the whole section in terms of how we see other people.

You will need to make the point that our state before we became Christians (and that of non-Christians now) was that we were:–

- *Dead* (v1). This is the result of transgressions and sins (these will need explaining)

- *Enslaved* (vv2–3), We were enslaved to the Devil, as he worked directly and also indirectly by using the world (that is, humanity organised without reference to God), and the flesh (that is, our fallen nature).

- *Disobedient* (v2). This is the essence of sin: we seek to take God's place and therefore disobey God.

- *Condemned* (v3) to the wrath of God.

You could draw out these points from small groups by asking them to fill out a doctor's report on a patient's condition from verses 1–3. The report could use headings such as 'symptoms', 'cause of illness', 'diagnosis', and 'prognosis'.

Half-time

Try this game:

Scrabble with a difference. Get hold of a Scrabble board (you won't need the tiles), and cut out sufficient squares of paper, or card, the same size as the squares to be adequate for a game of Scrabble. Write out a list of the values of the letters and put this on the wall for everyone to see. Split your group into two or more teams, and play 'Scrabble with a difference'. The difference is that although you only have seven squares at a time, *you* write the letters (and their scores) on to the blank pieces of paper or card, and you can only use words from the Bible passage (here Ephesians 2:1–10).

You can also do this game on an overhead projector.

Or . . .

Since this meeting is about God's work in saving us, ask one or two of your leaders or members to say how this happened for them. Ask people the week before, and if you are going to use an interview, tell them what questions you will ask. This could become a regular, but sporadic, part of your programme.

Second half

Read verses 4–10

These verses are about what God has done to save us. You may like to look at the verbs in order to explain what God has done.

More than this though, we see *why* God has intervened. He has acted in this way because of his character. God is a God of love (v4), mercy (v4), grace (vv5, 6, 8), and kindness (v7). It is because he is like this that he has acted in this way.

If you are using the doctor analogy from the First Half, you could continue it here (or start using it here), by asking groups to look at the treatment of the problem. Suggest that it is a disease, and so ask your group:

- 'What is the doctor like?'
- 'What is the treatment?'
- 'What do we need to prevent it recurring?'

Even verse 10, which seems to be about our response, is actually about God's purpose. He prepared the good works for us to do, and they are not something which we can contribute to our own salvation.

Right and Wrong. Split your group into teams of at least four and give each group a pile of cards, copied and cut up from the group extra page. Ask them to deal these out among the group. Then, as if playing cards, ask them to put one card at a time in the right, wrong or unsure column. These columns should be labelled using the extra card, also on the Group Extra page. When all cards are placed in the appropriate columns, members go round the group twice more and may move one card to a better place if they think it has been placed wrongly. The game should be conducted in silence, and then members may talk about it.

Group Extra

Right or Wrong?

a) RIGHT
b) WRONG
c) UNSURE

1. *The 'ruler of the kingdom of the air' is the Devil.*
2. *We were born under God's wrath.*
3. *Sin kills us.*
4. *We can boast about our salvation.*
5. *The Devil is at work in those who disobey God.*
6. *The Bible sometimes calls our sinful nature 'the flesh'.*
7. *Good works can save us.*

8. *Jesus reveals God's kindness.*
9. *What God did for Jesus he wants to do for us.*
10. *You must have faith to be saved.*
11. *Salvation is the gift of God.*
12. *God is not very merciful.*

Final whistle

Such a doctrinal passage, focusing on God's work, is hard to apply. Indeed, there is not the need to apply this as one would a more directly practical passage. But try this:

Praying in the passage. Explain the importance of thanksgiving in prayer, and show how it is possible by using very short prayers to thank God for what has done for us. These prayers should be firmly based on the passage. For example: 'Thank you Lord for your great love for us, Amen' (v4); 'Thank you that you are rich in mercy, Amen' (v4).

Extra time

(ie other ideas which could be used)

- If you played Guess Who? in the First Half you could to follow it up with further thought and prayer about non-Christian friends. Get into threes, and each person suggests the name of at least one friend. The group then prays for them, either aloud or quietly. This may also provide an incentive for further action in evangelism. Your group could pledge to talk to one friend about Christianity during the following week – and debrief next week to see how they are getting on.

- This is an excellent passage for an evangelisitic evening. You may like to invite someone to come and give an evangelistic talk, and make this evening just that little bit special.

Equipment

record cards
pen/pencil
newspapers (several copies of the same issue)
overhead projector and screen
copies of Group Extra
equipment for 'Scrabble with a difference'

Key Example 2

Ephesians 4:1–16: Unity and maturity

INTRODUCTION

This will be more use if you read the short introductory notes before preparing tomorrow's youth session using the programme outlined which follows.

Main teaching point

Again it can't be stressed enough that once this is clear, much of the application will flow naturally from this. Most of the work in preparing this teaching outline went into working on this main teaching point.

Strategy

This was maybe better left unsaid! Because a correct understanding of the church means that our young people are *bound* to apply it to how they get on with the rest of the church and not just other young people in the group.

Warm-up

To incorporate such a long (but very useful) game in a youth group evening will almost certainly mean that you will have to change the normal format of the evening to fit it in. Good! But most leaders will probably try to slot it into a standard evening without any compensation, and so upset the balance and rush the whole evening's programme.

First half/Second half

Both outline the meaning of the passage and then suggest presentation methods. Clearly the meaning of the passage is the same, but it can be taught in different ways.

Half-time

If you are doing the path building game and have therefore re-arranged the evening, the prayer web is a different way of conducting the prayer time.

Second half

The use of drawing will help the young people to think about the teaching and apply it to their lives, although they probably won't realize they are doing it!

Final whistle

Helps with this application, and arises directly from the passage. It is aimed to help young people think about how the passage applies to them without being directive (ie It avoids saying 'You must do this because the Bible says so').

THE SESSION

Teaching point

Christian maturity results from the use of the diversity of gifts within the church.

Group Action

To recognise the gifts they have and use these to help the church grow to maturity.

Briefing

This week's passage is about the church. It would be easy to apply the lessons to your group and how they get on with each other, and by all means to that. But do not miss out on this valuable opportunity to teach and challenge your young people about their commitment to the church as a whole.

Warm-up

Try this warm up game. Although it is lengthy, it is worth it.

Path Building. Copy and cut up the cards from the Group Extra sheet and hand them out to your group members. There are thirty-three cards, so you may need to give more than one to each person, or share. This does not matter.

Group members must not show their cards to anyone else. Working as a team, ask your group to work out the date the path is completed. Time them. This can be done in twelve minutes, so stop them after about twenty-five minutes. The correct answer is 8th June. It is best if they work out a calendar and then calculate from this when each stage is completed. Suggest this if they get stuck.

At the end, debrief. Find out about their feelings. Make comments on people's attitudes: who joined in and who did not. Make the point that every card was vital and therefore every persons' contribution was crucial if the answer was to be found out. Ask what happened when people opted out.

Ask your group in what ways this parallels the church, and then explain that this meeting is about the church.

Group Extra

Instruction cards for *Build a Path*

All concrete and tools are delivered on Thursday 4th April.

Today is Monday 1st April

The path is 100 metres long.

It takes 4 people to lay the path. No work can be done if only 3 people are present.

Peter is ill on Sunday 12th May and can't help lay the path on that day.

Hard core can't be delivered until Wednesday 24th April.

It rains on Friday 3rd May.

Peter has to go to a wedding all day on Saturday 20th April.

4 people work 10 hours a day on the path.

It rains on Saturday 18th May.

Peter is ill on Sunday 26th May and can't help lay the path.

No work on the path can be done either on the day when it rains, or on the day after it rains.

It rains on Friday 17th May.

The path is made of concrete with a hard core foundation.

John has ample money to buy supplies.

Sarah can only work on the path for 3 weekends a month (any 3 weekends).

John can only work on the path at weekends.

Peter can work on the path at any time.

Work can start as soon as everyone is available.

Ian can work on the path at any time.

John, Peter, Sarah and Ian are all good friends living in the same town, and except where stated can be quickly and easily available to lay the path.

The only people who work on the path are John, Peter, Sarah and Ian.

The path is laid in 3 stages: (1) preparation of the ground, (2) hard core foundation, (3) concrete top layer.

It takes 2 people 5 hours to lay 10 metres of hard core.

The four people work in pairs on the hard core foundation.

All the hard core foundation has to be complete before any concrete is laid.

Once the hard core is finished, the 4 people take the rest of the day off.

It takes the 4 people all working together 2 hours to prepare 5 metres of ground for the path.

All the preparation of the ground has to be complete before the hard core foundation is laid.

All 4 must work together to lay the concrete.

It takes the people 5 hours to lay 10 metres of concrete.

All the ground has to be prepared before the path is laid. All the hard core has to be laid before any concrete can be put down.

John is wanting to build a path. He needs 3 friends to help him.

Some of my gifts

Possible gifts

1 2 3 4 5 6 7 8 9 10
1 2 3 4 5 6 7 8 9 10
1 2 3 4 5 6 7 8 9 10
1 2 3 4 5 6 7 8 9 10
1 2 3 4 5 6 7 8 9 10
1 2 3 4 5 6 7 8 9 10
1 2 3 4 5 6 7 8 9 10
1 2 3 4 5 6 7 8 9 10
1 2 3 4 5 6 7 8 9 10
1 2 3 4 5 6 7 8 9 10
1 2 3 4 5 6 7 8 9 10
1 2 3 4 5 6 7 8 9 10
1 2 3 4 5 6 7 8 9 10
1 2 3 4 5 6 7 8 9 10
1 2 3 4 5 6 7 8 9 10
1 2 3 4 5 6 7 8 9 10
1 2 3 4 5 6 7 8 9 10
1 2 3 4 5 6 7 8 9 10
1 2 3 4 5 6 7 8 9 10

Kick-off

Kick off by reminding your group that Ephesians 4 is at the start of
the second half of Ephesians. Chapters 1–3 deal with doctrine,
with God's action, and with details about our salvation. The
second half of Ephesians starts here and covers our duty, our
reaction, and how salvation works out in practice.

It would be a good start to review the sessions on Ephesians so
far. You could do this informally, in open discussion, trying to get
your group to remember the main teaching points from Ephesians

1–3. It would help to jog their memories if you dig out the audio-visual aids and jokes you used.

Then, having put Ephesians 4:1-6 in context, explain that in the church we have a lot in common with each other (see vv4-6). But the church also has a great variety and diversity. God wants us to use the variety of gifts in the church so that we all grow as Christians.

First half

Ask someone to read all of Ephesians 4:1-16. As a break from the usual, try asking one person to stand and read it all, with a light behind them and the rest of the room in darkness. Or ask your group to stand while the reader sits to read. Or have the reader sit at the back and read. Or pre-record it with some faint background music. Use your imagination!

Both First Half and Second Half will look at the whole passage, and both teach that Christian maturity is brought about by the church as a whole, using their gifts. First Half will focus on verses 1–13 in particular.

In verse 1, 'a life worthy of the calling you have received' is a mature Christian life. This is unpacked a little more in verses 2 and 3. Note from verse 3 that we do not create unity. The Holy Spirit does that. Our responsibility is to strive (work as hard as we can) to keep it, and this is primarily within *our* church before we think of unity between churches. Moreover, Christian unity is possible only because God is one (verses 4–5). The unity of Ephesians 4:1–6 is based on the fact that the people of God have so much in common. And God's people are meant to be growing to Christian maturity.

But how do we grow to this Christian maturity? Through the use of gifts in the church. We all have been given grace (v7), and there is a wide variety of gifts in the church (v11). The reason for these gifts is that God's people should be prepared for service so that they will be built up and become mature in their faith (v13).

You may want to do a short talk (no more than ten minutes) to cover these points.

Alternatively, in groups of three, ask these three questions:

- Verse 1. What is a life 'worthy of the calling you have received'?

- Verses 3–6. What do we have in common with others in the church? What do we learn about unity in the church?

- Verses 11–13. Why do we have different gifts in the church?

In the comeback (either after each question or after all three), explain that as a church we have much in common with each other. We have a variety of gifts, and we need to use these gifts in the church to produce Christian maturity.

To highlight the diversity and its importance in the church, ask your group to name four different types of people who come to church (eg babies, bikers, grandmas, executives, teenagers), and for each grouping, ask your young people to come up with two unique characteristics of each which are valuable to the church.

Half-time

Try one of the following. The Prayer Web is a good way of introducing your prayer time.

The Prayer Web. Ask your group to stand round in one big circle (or, if you have a very large group, then several separate circles of ten to twelve people). Taking a large ball of string/wool/cotton, joint the circle. Holding on to the end of the string, mention one thing you would like to pray for, and then toss the ball to someone else in the circle. The person who catches the ball says something else that they would like to pray for, holds on to the string and throws it on to someone else, and so on until you have spun a web. Pray for these things.

When you have prayed, stay where you are and begin to ask the group what the string represented.

- What's it doing?
- What happens if it's cut?
- What happens if someone lets go?

Do not take the analogy too far, but draw out the facts that we are bound together and belong together as Christians. Broken relationships and absentees harm all the church – we need each other.

Human Frogs. This game is a bit like the church, because it only works when everyone joins in. Divide your group into three. One section sings in a high staccato sound: 'Tomatoes, tomatoes, tomatoes'. One section sings more slowly in alto or tenor: 'Potatoes, potatoes, potatoes'. One section sings in a slow low bass: 'Fried bacon, fried bacon, fried bacon'. Rehearse separately, and then all join together to produce the sound of croaking frogs.

Second half

This focuses on verses 14-16. You may like to re-read them, but first recap what you discovered in First Half.

These verses paint two pictures, one of an immature church, and one of a mature church. The immature church, with immature Christians, is unable to tell true from false teaching, and so are tossed around theologically (v14). They are unstable.

The church which is growing to maturity (v15–16) deals with false teaching by speaking the truth in love, and grows up spiritually to become more and more like Jesus. He is the hub of the church, holding the whole people together as 'each part does its work' (that is, as all Christians use their gifts to build up the church). It is a stable church.

You could ask your group individually to draw a picture which represents one of these situations. This should help your young people to think about the two situations, and how they could be portrayed.

Alternatively, if you are gifted in this area (or someone else in your church is), make a drawing yourself and have it displayed throughout the meeting, or give it to members as a handout.

If you really are not in the slightest bit artistic (but you should not let that put you off here!), divide your group into two. Ask each half to look at the infant church and the mature church. Look at the characteristics, and decide which you are. Put instructions for this up on an OHP or wallchart, and in the comeback, match their replies with your own personal study of the passages.

Final Whistle

Here we want to help our members see what their gifts are and how they can contribute in order to help the church grow to maturity and therefore unity. Try one or both of these:

(a) Use the 'Some of my gifts' section of the Group Extra sheet. First ask group members to fill in the spaces to the left of each row with possible gifts that people might have. Start with those in verse 11. Add other really mundane ones, and ask your group to add more, up to twenty. Then they should give themselves a score out of ten as to how good they think they are at this particular ability. Then pick a friend and do the same for them. Suggest that their higher scores are things which they could work at in the church, and ask them to tell their friend what they reckon their friend's higher scores are.

(b) This could follow on from (a). Ask your group members to list five talents/gifts/offerings which they could give to help the church grow to maturity. Explain that even the smallest thing is very important, and that although it may not help directly, our small help can contribute to releasing people like the teachers who can help the church to grow to maturity more directly. Having listed the five areas, for each one ask your group members to say how they will make their offering/use their gift this coming week, and to say when they will do this. They need to be specific!

Suggest that group members then pick one particular thing which they can focus on during this coming week. But be specific – get them to decide precisely what they will do, and when they will do it. Tell them too what you are going to do, and when!

Memory verse

Ephesians 4:15 'Instead, speaking the truth in love, we will in all things grow up into him who is the head, that is, Christ.'

Equipment

Copies of the Group Extra sheets
Large ball of string
Pens, paper
OHP/screen or large sheet of paper
Drawings for Second Half

Extra Time

Two other games which you may find helpful:

Potato Tower. In teams of four, ask your group to build the highest tower possible with potatoes and cocktail stocks. It adds an element of fun to do it in silence, and it's more instructive. Make sure you debrief with questions about how it felt, what they learned, what parallels there are with the church.

One Body. Divide up into groups of four. Within each four, one person should be the eyes, one the mouth, one the right hand, and one the left hand. For the purposes of this game each person can only use that part of the anatomy which they are. So everyone closes their eyes apart from the eyes, only the mouth can speak, etc. Ask the groups to practise being what they are, and then say you are about to put an object in the middle of the group. The aim is to unwrap it, and place one of the contents into the mouth. Place a tube of sweets in the middle of the group, and say 'Go'.

Debrief on feelings, what they learned about working together, what they learned about the church.

5

Putting it Together and Keeping it Together – Constructing a Teaching Evening

'I know the evening service went on a bit, but they shouldn't still be going at 10.30.' Meanwhile, as parents shivered in the cold outside the church hall, the youth leader struggled to explain another meaningless game. The programme was two-thirds of the way through, and they just had to get to the end, where the application exercise was just out of this world. So out of this world that it had nothing to do with what they were supposed to be learning, and was actually impossible to do in such a small church hall. Thankfully, one bold parent interjected . . .

This chapter aims to help us to avoid getting into the situation described above. Now that you have worked out what you are going to say, how do you say it? Of all the hundreds of possible ways of getting across the information, how do we decide which to use?

Musts and Maybes

We've studied the passage and we know what to say. Now is the time to decide how to say it. In any teaching evening there is a vast choice of different methods of doing this, but there are essential elements and optional ones: 'Musts' and 'Maybes'.

Musts

Communicating what the passage says is one thing that *must* be done. Whatever else we do, this must be covered every time. Sometimes we jump straight to application without considering what the passage said in the first place. Sometimes we are terribly academic, studying what the passage says, but never able to communicate its application to our young people. And sometimes we ignore what the Bible is saying, and merely entertain members with:

Maybes

These are elements which could be in the evening's programme, but they are optional, and it would not be catastrophic if we decided against including any of them. They aren't essential.

We need to consider the Musts and the Maybes both in the preparation and at the meeting itself. When preparing, we need to decide what we plan to leave in. At the meeting we need to be prepared to leave material out. But both in the planning and at the meeting, the criteria for leaving material in or out are the same: is it a Must or Maybe?

For example, at the last minute we may decide against using an ice-breaker which we had prepared because they are relaxing well over coffee, and time is getting short.

We may decide against using a relaxing game in the middle of the meeting because the group's enthusiasm and concentration are at a high level.

In our planning we may decide against using a more raucous role play because one of our members has just had a family bereavement and the group just won't be in the mood for it.

In our planning we come across a good game about the church which would be brilliant if there is time to include it. So we note it down, and come prepared, but in the event we run out of time, and the only one disappointed about it is us – no-one else knows.

These are all optional elements; we don't have to use them in the meeting. In each case there is no loss from deciding to drop them. They are 'Maybes'.

And in fact there is a positive gain.

It's very easy to be conned into thinking that we must have this game or that activity in order to make the meeting go well, and so we try and weave it in, even when it's totally inappropriate – and optional.

More than that, it's easy to feel that we must make the Bible come alive by our presentation methods. The Bible *is* alive. It *is* active. 'The word of God is living and active. Sharper than any double-edged sword, it penetrates even to dividing soul and spirit, joints and marrow; it judges the thoughts, and attitudes of the heart' (Hebrews 4:12). Presentation ideas merely help young people to understand something which is by nature, living, active, and powerful.

Decisions, decisions . . . how to decide on what to do

It's all very well having a stockpile of brilliant ideas, and knowing what's a Must and what's a Maybe, but how do we actually decide which Maybes to use?

The following may help.

- **Teaching the point.** Does this game activity/idea/method actually get across the point we want to make? This is vital. If it *almost* teaches it but doesn't actually do so, think again! Be absolutely clear about what it is that you are trying to teach, and about what the chosen method will communicate.

- **Can we cope?** Think of the other leaders and yourself: do you have the expertise and experience to lead this item? Do you understand how to run the activity? Have you thought out possible pitfalls? If you are going to lead a review session, it's far easier if you have been at all the sessions you are reviewing. Some complicated simulation games need a competent leader who knows the game backwards, and has preferably played it before.

- **What about our group?** Is the group too big or too small for this activity? Would they actually do it or is it 'beneath' them? Would they enjoy it? Would they get the point if they did do it? Will they be dressed suitably?

- **Available resources – can we get hold of them?** Don't plan to use an overhead projector, a flip chart, VCR or television unless you are absolutely sure that the equipment is available, and you know how to use it. And what happens if it breaks down? Always have a 'Plan B' up your sleeve.

- **Where are we meeting?** Can we really have a toothpaste race in our living room? Are there curtains or a blackout for slides? Are there tables for playing Scrabble with a Difference?

- **Finances.** It's good to have visiting speakers occasionally (no matter how small your group is), but are there finances to pay the speaker's travelling expenses? It would be nice too to be able to give them a little something for coming. Finances are useful for other things too – like photocopying, video hire, etc. Your church ought to give your group a regular grant to cover running expenses. Youth groups cost money, but many churches, think they can run on fresh air.

- **Time.** Some excellent teaching methods take a lot of time. Simulation games and role plays can be very time-consuming, especially if you are going to do a proper debrief afterwards. It may be that you simply don't have the time for these. Or perhaps you will have to drop the singing for this week, or start earlier, or have a special meeting. We *do* need to watch the clock. Not only is boredom deadly, but we have also got a responsibility to member's parents to get their children home in good time.

- **Relevance.** Is a chosen method suitable for what you want to teach? For example if the subject is the Second Coming, make the meeting unpredictable – which the Second Coming is!

- **Variety.** Was this idea used last week or the week before? It's good to maintain variety within and between meetings. The same brilliant idea three weeks running somehow loses its shine. So keep a record of what has been done, and avoid that TV disease – the repeat.

- **Is it safe?** We can't be too careful. One published ice-breaker I came across consisted of putting safety pins in others' clothes while preventing others pinning them on you! Who's your lawyer?

  Also, ask if a potential method is emotionally safe. Don't, for example, play games which look for the person with the largest nose or the smelliest feet, unless of course you are sure that you would win hands down!

- **Is it foolproof?** Will they see ways round the rules? I dreamed up one game for our youth group which they demolished within thirty seconds by finding a gaping loophole I had totally missed. Show new games to other leaders for comment before launching them. Somehow young people have the knack of torpedoing the most apparently seaworthy of new ideas . . .

Staying on track – Matching our methods with the message

A youth group teaching evening is a very complex event. There are all sorts of different things going on. There's a vast amount of communication happening – verbal and non-verbal – between the leaders and the members, and between members and other members. Let's focus briefly on what we are saying to them by our choice of teaching method – or at least what *they* think we are saying to them.

- If we use chalk and talk, they'll probably think Christianity is like school.

- If we use an ice-breaker, they'll see that Christianity can be fun.

- If we're serious about the Bible, they'll see it's a book to be respected and read.

- If we use group work, they'll begin to see how we can help each other to learn.

- If we use straightforward teaching, they'll begin to see the power of the word of God simply explained, and grow in confidence in the word. Have a look at 2 Corinthians 4:2:

  > Rather, we have renounced secret and shameful ways; we do not use deception, nor do we distort the word of God. On the contrary, by setting forth the truth plainly we commend ourselves to every man's conscience in the sight of God (2 Corinthians 4:2).

It's easy to use inappropriate methods. For instance giving a straight talk on the church, would be less appropriate than the group working on something *together*, where the input of everyone is vital. Bringing along a whole pile of paper for a game on the environment, also contradicts the teaching of the evening.

By contrast an Australian evening, or a back-to-front evening, when considering the kingdom of God, is a good way of illustrating how the kingdom of God turns upside down the values of the world around. The Australian evening could start with a short snatch of 'Neighbours' or 'Home and Away', be decorated by (empty) cans of Fosters or XXXX (or posters for them), be taken in Australian accents, adorned by Australian tee shirts, amused by Crocodile Dundee videos, and taught using notes given out on green and gold paper.

The back-to-front evening begins by saying goodbye, reverses the normal running order, has the chairs facing the back, coffee in the wrong place, the overhead projector back to front (at least initially), and ends with you saying, Hello! It's nice to see you!

Having only decaffeinated coffee and tea and no Coke in an evening on drugs reinforces the point. Giving the group a chance to give during an evening on giving, fleshes out the message they are hearing. To help us to be careful and sensitive, and to have more of an integrated package, consider three things:

- **The message.** What do you want to say? Always come back to this. Keep on asking 'Are they getting the message?'

  - **The Methods.** Do they help to teach the message? Do they support it? What is the method *itself* actually saying?

    - **The Members.** Try and put yourself in their shoes, and ask what they think of the method – not just whether they enjoy it or not. Ask what kind of values they think the activity is portraying.

Variety is the spice of . . . keeping variety in the teaching programme

Work hard to maintain variety rather than induce a coma by doing the same thing or the same *sort* of thing, week in week out. Here are some ideas for adding a bit of spice:

- **Keep a record.** My group are better than I am at remembering what we have done. So I now keep a record to avoid repeating myself. I also keep a note of what they did and didn't like.

- **Keep a lookout.** Always be on the lookout for new ideas so that the input into your store of ideas exceeds the output. Flick through books of ideas which you come across in Christian bookshops, or on displays at conferences, and see what's around.

- **Use the leaders.** We need a variety of *people* as well as a variety of ideas in our group meetings. The same method introduced by different people often doesn't *feel* quite the same. In the Bible, leadership is always plural. Use all (both?) of your leaders regularly in the teaching sessions, or invite your minister for an evening.

- **Visitors.** Visiting speakers are great value. Ask other members of your church, your friends, or see if your minister has people he can suggest. Try the other churches in town, or in a nearby village. Have a joint meeting occasionally with another youth group, and join with their leaders in doing the teaching.

- **Training.** Training events provide new ideas. They come from the up-front speakers, other delegates and from recommended new resources on display or for sale.

- **New ideas.** Get yourself on the mailing list of a national youth organisation. Some have regular mailings which include the latest presentation ideas.

- **Adapt.** When you watch the television or listen to the radio, ask yourself whether what you are seeing or hearing could be adapted for your youth group. Think of using secular sources of games and activities – for instance, Trivial Pursuits could be adapted, so could Monopoly, Cluedo or Pictionary.

- **Change for change's sake.** Look at the last programme and decide what can be changed. Maybe it's the place you meet at, or perhaps the time of the meeting. Perhaps it's the style of the programme card, or the people who teach. It could be the structure of the meeting, or anything else. Ask of all these how they could be changed. Maybe meet at 8.00 am on a Sunday instead of 8.00 pm! Meet somewhere different. Introduce proper coffee; have a meal; drop the singing; vary how you pray; have an extra short meeting, and so on. Change almost everything occasionally – apart, that is, from the one thing which

we aren't at liberty to change at all: our responsibility to teach
our young people the Bible. But change with care. Young people
are surprisingly conservative and many resent change. So don't
change everything all the time. Indeed it's probably better to
change nothing most of the time.

Remember, though, at the end of all this, that the variety of
presentation ideas isn't the be-all and end-all. There are plenty of
ideas, books and training events which provide ideas. But these are
short-term needs, and our overall long-term aim is to be teaching
and discipling our young people so that they become Christians
and grow to Christian maturity.

If you are teaching consecutive passages, variety is still
important, but a quick review is vital to see how the present passage
fits in with the previous one. The major single reason why people
misunderstand the Bible is because they don't look at it in context.

So, for instance, Jeremiah 29 has that much-loved passage in verse
11: 'For I know the plans I have for you', declares the Lord, 'plans to
prosper you and not to harm you, plans to give you hope and a
future.' We love to pick this out, putting it on a notice board or
memory verse card, or making it our motto for the year. But it
actually makes far more sense if you read the first ten verses of
Jeremiah 29, which reveal that it's part of a letter written by Jeremiah
(in Jerusalem) to Jews (in Babylon) during the exile, assuring them
that their situation is not hopeless, because the future of the people
of Israel lies with them and not those in Jerusalem.

Context is vital.

Also remember that youth leaders teach by example. Skills like
handling the Bible are caught as well as taught – caught as we teach
the young people and as they catch on to our way of handling
Scripture.

Each week I meet with one of the older boys in our youth group
and we read the Bible together, just the two of us. In recent weeks I
have been thrilled at how he is learning to read the Bible for
himself, to ask the right questions of the passage, to look at the
context and to draw out the main points. I haven't taught him that
formally, but he has picked it up as we have gone along, and he is
now passing it on to others.

Every now and then it may be a good idea to review what you've done over a whole term. It is best to give this a good billing, a 'Rave Review', because on the outside it doesn't seem terribly attractive. But such sessions can be enormous fun, and very helpful to you. That's because they give the opportunity to

- see how well we've communicated with our group members.
- re-do anything we have done badly.
- check understanding and re-explain points which haven't been completely understood.
- see how the application is going, and whether the Bible is in fact making a difference in the lives of our young people.

We can make these sessions fun by doing things like cracking the same jokes, but getting the young people to provide the punch line, by bringing out old audio-visual aids and handouts, or by doing one or two of the best activities again. Have a 'read and chips' evening, where you read through all that you have done, then break for chips, and then come back to discuss what it all means. Meet somewhere different, or incorporate it into a weekend away.

The Key Examples show how this can work out in practice.

As you review recent group sessions, don't ignore the need to review your own work. Every so often (the end of a short series is a suitable time) look back and ask questions like:

'How well did we do?'
'How well did we communicate God's word?'
'What were the good points?'
'What were the bad points?'
'What should be avoided in the future?'
'How can we build on our good points and make them even better?'
'What did members like and dislike?'

Looking back is the key to forward thinking.

Be a confident leader

a) Be bold

You can do it!

There is a huge number of youth workers with an unnecessary inferiority complex when they compare themselves with other youth leaders. But being a youth leader isn't all about stunning up-front escapades and dazzling Sunday evening programmes. The heart of the matter is spending time with a few members, getting to know them, and letting the Christian faith be communicated from your slightly older Christian life to theirs. Don't be intimidated by super hero youth leaders, and don't try and imitate them. We need to be ourselves, but also try out occasional new ideas. Be bold!

b) Know your group

This is important in youth work, and it takes time. It takes time to get to know them, and for them to get to know you. But as you do get to know your group, the selection and adaptation of ideas becomes easier. You get to know what would work and what wouldn't. You understand what they like and what they don't. You work out the best ways of communicating God's truth to your young people.

c) Know your task

Your task is to understand the passage you are teaching and then communicate this clearly to the group members, using appropriate methods. Therefore, when selecting and adapting ideas, know what it *is* you are trying to communicate, and think carefully about the methods, asking whether they will actually communicate what the passage is saying. 'Almost but not quite; isn't quite good enough.

You may be able to refine the method so it will teach the passage, but if you can't, it's better to ditch the idea altogether rather than have something which almost, but doesn't quite, work.

Being a youth leader can be a very frustrating business. One of the most frustrating things is having to discard a lot of good ideas because they aren't quite on target. It's also a good exercise in self-discipline.

d) Know your circumstances

Many youth groups I come across are small (say, less than ten). Most books of ideas assume that the group is much bigger. So most of us will have to ask questions such as these about a prospective teaching method:

> • Can I do this with a group of four? If so, how?
> • How can I make it less boisterous, so that we can do it in our living room?
> • It's far too long. How can I prune it?
> • It's far too expensive. Are there cheaper substitutes?

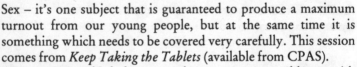

Key Example One

Sex – Whose bright idea was it anyway?

INTRODUCTION

Sex – it's one subject that is guaranteed to produce a maximum turnout from our young people, but at the same time it is something which needs to be covered very carefully. This session comes from *Keep Taking the Tablets* (available from CPAS).

You may not think that you and/or your group could cope with the smile test, so stick with the newspaper search which draws the group's attention to the number of references to sex, male/female relationships etc., which are in the media today. The published resource doesn't suggest which newspaper to use, but it may be wise to avoid certain publications! Alternatively, you could compare the coverage of, say, *The Times*, with that of the *Daily Express*. The Milk Tray prize could be embellished by presenting it by a hero dashing in all dressed in black . . .

Focus

This narrows in on individuals, and keeps the initial answers secret while making individuals consider their own thoughts and attitudes. It may be too much to have this and the warm up, so choose one or the other.

Bible 1

This is very important. It is the core of the evening, together with Bible 2 – it's a Must rather than a Maybe. So don't let it get squeezed by the other activities. It's possible to do this as a straight talk (and quicker, if you are well prepared and don't waffle), but also useful to get members finding out things for themselves.

Assimilate

The value of having outside speakers or visitors is underlined here. If you have two leaders you could do this. Think carefully over the value of members getting to know leaders against the drawbacks of not taking the opportunity to get visitors in.

'Bible 2'

This contains a problem-solving exercise which applies the findings of 'Bible 1', and involves a report back within a small group. It's always good to vary the group size, especially for different activities during a teaching evening.

Reinforce

See the footnote after 'Reinforce'. This is a big and important subject for teenagers, and points to the need for careful programme planning to incorporate advice like this into the programme as it is being planned.

THE SESSION

Aim to teach that

Sex is a precious and exciting gift of God – His Spirit can direct our sexuality and our marriages to produce the greatest fulfilment.

Aim that the group should

Learn to discuss sex and similar subjects with mature and helpful openness.

Equipment Needed

Item	*Section*
Enough copies of the same newspaper for every third member of the group to have one	1(b)
Similar number of felt-tip pens or highlighters	1(b)
Box of Milk Tray as prize	1(b)
GROUP EXTRA The Ideal Partner (page 25) for each member and pens/biros	2
Mars Bar for prize	2
GROUP EXTRA (page 26) for each member	3
GROUP EXTRA (pages 27 & 28) A Question of Friendships for each member	5

Warm-up (5 mins)

(a) Smile Contest

Ask everyone to sit in a circle. Choose one person to be 'it'. He/she picks someone in the circle and sits on his or her lap. He/she then says, 'if you love me, sweetheart, smile.'

The person who is being sat upon must say, 'I love you, sweetheart, but I just can't smile.' If he/she laughs, or even smiles, he/she becomes 'it'. Stop the game at an appropriate moment.

And/or

(b) Newspaper Search

Divide into groups of three or four. Give each group a felt-tip pen or highlighter and a copy of the same newspaper. Each group is to mark as many references as they can find to male/female relationships, marriage, sex, advertisements that use sex, etc. The team with the most after five minutes wins. (Milk Tray as a prize).

Focus (10 mins)

The Ideal Partner

Give each member a copy of the Quality Choice competition sheet (GROUP EXTRA). They fill in the second column with their order of importance numbering from 1–11 the qualities listed in the first column, having added a further quality at the bottom of the list, if they like.

Then in the third column, they give the leader marks out of 10 for his/her own qualities.

Finally, they complete the slogan for the ideal partner: 'I think the most important quality is . . . because . . . '

The sheets are collected and a leader decides the winner of the Mars Bar!

Bible input One (12 mins)

Read out Exodus 20:14. Explain the meaning of adultery: God created man and woman to be together in a permanent exclusive relationship of one man with one woman (the polygamous – more than one wife – marriages of the Old Testament are pictures of unhappiness and strife: Sarah and Hagar, Rachel and Leah, Hannah and Peninnah etc.). This is a sexual relationship. Outside

FOOTNOTE

By and large the group will benefit if the leader(s) are prepared to invite some gentle mockery. This can be valuable to show that you do not take yourself too seriously, that you are aware of your own idiosyncrasies, and that you are vulnerable to the group's opinions. The moment when the leader feels weakest and most humiliated can sometimes be the moment that he or she gets through to the group best.

marriage sexual intercourse is called fornication, and across marriage it is called adultery. The Bible bans both.

Divide into two groups, to tackle two separate tasks. Group 1 to study Genesis 1:27, 28; Genesis 2:18–25; 1 Corinthians 6:15–20 and to find as many reasons as you can from those bible passages why God created sex. Group 2 to study Genesis 2:18–25; Matthew 19:4–6; 1 Corinthians 7:3–5; and to answer the question 'What are God's guidelines for a good marriage?' from those passages.

These group tasks and verses are written out in GROUP EXTRA, which can be photocopied and given to each member of the group. Ask each group to record their findings with the appropriate bible verse. After five minutes bring the two groups back together again, and ask a spokesman from each group to report back to the other group.

Assimilate (16 mins)

Marriage – Warts and all

A married couple, who are mature and confident, with a stable marriage and a good sense of humour, should talk for 10 minutes on the realities of married life. This will need to be carefully prepared and frank, dealing openly with the things that have created the greatest strain in the marriage. Look over all your church (and elsewhere if necessary!) to find the right couple. It is important not to miss out this section.

Divide into two groups by sex, and give each group (the boys and the girls) four minutes to discuss together and formulate one question they would like to ask the married couple. Then get each sex to put their question to the couple.

FOOTNOTE

In this sort of exercise encourage the groups to list their findings in an ordered sequence: 'We found four reasons why God created sex: first . . .' It is important that you yourself know the main teaching of these passages on the topic in question. After each report-back you can invite comments and contributions from the whole group, and at that point you or another leader can volunteer anything significant that they have missed. The 1 Corinthians passages in particular will need careful attention and will require good understanding on the leader's part. Look at a good commentary beforehand.

GROUP EXTRA 3

PLAY

QUALITY CHOICE

WIN A MARS BAR!

QUALITIES		
LOOKS		
AGE		
WEIGHT		
~~Intel Intellig~~ CLEVERNESS		
PERSONALITY		
WEALTH		
MATURITY		
SMELL		
PRAYER-LIFE		
DRESS-SENSE		

NOW COMPLETE THIS SLOGAN USING A MAXIMUM OF 25 WORDS

THE MOST IMPORTANT QUALITY FOR THE IDEAL PARTNER IS _____

BECAUSE _____

FOOTNOTE

You can 'personalise' this page of GROUP EXTRA by adding your own name, or another leader's, or a well-established group member's, in the blanks in the first paragraph. It would also be wise to read the page carefully and decide whether there is a fictional name there which might give offence in the content of your group. If there is, simply blank it out and insert an appropriately unknown name instead!

This is on the wrong page

sp.

Bible input Two (15 mins)

A Question of Friendships

Pass out copies of the script (GROUP EXTRA).

Explain to the group that this passage describes a fictitious youth group, and that they are in a position to advise any single member described in the story. Divide them into pairs. Suggest they read through the narrative together, decide which of the members they would most like to help, and then hunt through the bible verses to find something they can share with him or her.

After eight minutes in pairs, bring four pairs together into groups to report back to one another.

Reinforce (8 mins)

Briefly recapitulate the main points that have arisen during the session. In particular, try to emphasize the specific lessons in Bible 2 for your group. Then have a time of quiet to reflect on lessons learnt.

Have a prayer time, led by one of the leaders, of thanksgiving for sexuality, confession of failure and thanks for God's forgiveness. Don't ask a group member to lead this.

Revise Matthew 5:44, and learn 1 Corinthians 6:19–20 'You do not belong to yourselves but to God; He bought you for a price'.

FOOTNOTE

To save embarrassment it is important not only to be familiar with, but also to be excited by, the bible's teaching on sex. You may not want to offend the sensibilities of the group, but it is very important to be unshockable. The members probably discuss sex with their contemporaries very frankly and explicitly. It is helpful if all issues of sex and sexuality (which we often find embarrassing), such as contraception and masturbation, are aired sensible in a Christian forum. Firm, frank, sensible, unshockable leadership is needed.

Music suggestions

Abba Father, let me be	MP 1
I am weak, but Thou art strong	MP 82
What a friend we have in Jesus	MP 262

FOOTNOTE

If members of your group have reading difficulties, it would be better for someone to read passages aloud while they follow in their own copies. Do be sensitive to the less academically able members of your group. De-emphasize academic ability as an important value within the group.

This subject obviously needs longer than just one teaching session for a teenage group. If the group only do this one session, they will not have covered it adequately. Two other possibilities are to expand it into two sessions, or to run a longer session than usual by starting in the early evening and breaking to eat together. Some group members might find it easier to talk on this subject in the more informal setting of a meal. You could then finish the session afterwards, ending at your normal time.

If you decide to have an unstructured time, it can be valuable to do part of that in single sex groups. The need for sympathetic, unshockable and mature leadership remains.

GROUP EXTRA 3

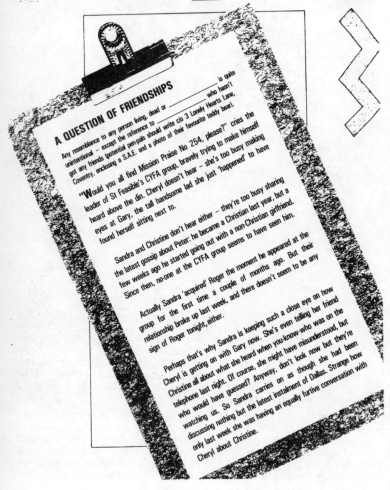

A QUESTION OF FRIENDSHIPS

Any resemblance to any person living, dead or _____ is quite unintentional – except the reference to _____ who hasn't got any friends (potential pen-pals should write c/o 3 Lonely Hearts Lane, Coventry, enclosing a S.A.E. and a photo of their favourite teddy bear).

"Would you all find Mission Praise No 254, please?" cries the leader of St Feasible's CYFA group, bravely trying to make himself heard above the din. Cheryl doesn't hear – she's too busy making eyes at Gary, the tall handsome lad she just 'happened' to have found herself sitting next to.

Sandra and Christine don't hear either – they're too busy sharing the latest gossip about Peter: he became a Christian last year, but a few weeks ago he started going out with a non-Christian girlfriend. Since then, no-one at the CYFA group seems to have seen him.

Actually Sandra 'acquired' Roger the moment he appeared at the group for the first time a couple of months ago. But their relationship broke up last week, and there doesn't seem to be any sign of Roger tonight, either.

Perhaps that's why Sandra is keeping such a close eye on how Cheryl is getting on with Gary now. She's even telling her friend Christine all about what she heard when you-know-who was on the telephone last night. Of course, she might have misunderstood, but who would have guessed? Anyway, don't look now but they're watching us. So Sandra carries on as though she had been discussing nothing but the latest instalment of Dallas. Strange how only last week she was having an equally furtive conversation with Cheryl about Christine.

GROUP E XTRA 3

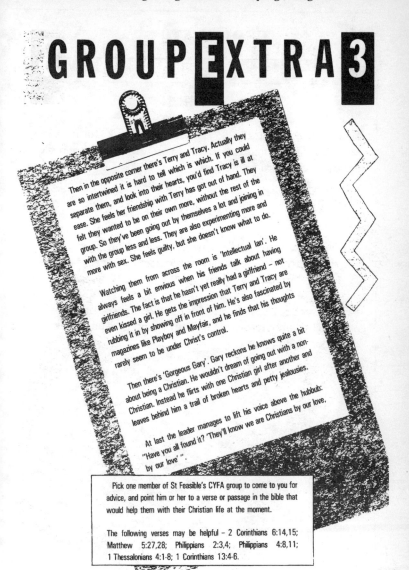

Then in the opposite corner there's Terry and Tracy. Actually they are so intertwined it is hard to tell which is which. If you could separate them, and look into their hearts, you'd find Tracy is ill at ease. She feels her friendship with Terry has got out of hand. They felt they wanted to be on their own more, without the rest of the group. So they've been going out by themselves a lot and joining in with the group less and less. They are also experimenting more and more with sex. She feels guilty, but she doesn't know what to do.

Watching them from across the room is 'Intellectual Ian'. He always feels a bit envious when his friends talk about having girlfriends. The fact is that he hasn't yet really had a girlfriend – not even kissed a girl. He gets the impression that Terry and Tracy are rubbing it in by showing off in front of him. He's also fascinated by magazines like Playboy and Mayfair, and he finds that his thoughts rarely seem to be under Christ's control.

Then there's 'Gorgeous Gary'. Gary reckons he knows quite a bit about being a Christian. He wouldn't dream of going out with a non-Christian. Instead he flirts with one Christian girl after another and leaves behind him a trail of broken hearts and petty jealousies.

At last the leader manages to lift his voice above the hubbub: "Have you all found it? 'They'll know we are Christians by our love, by our love' ".

Pick one member of St Feasible's CYFA group to come to you for advice, and point him or her to a verse or passage in the bible that would help them with their Christian life at the moment.

The following verses may be helpful – 2 Corinthians 6:14,15; Matthew 5:27,28; Philippians 2:3,4; Philippians 4:8,11; 1 Thessalonians 4:1-8; 1 Corinthians 13:4-6.

GROUP EXTRA 3

GROUP 1

Look at Genesis 1:27–28; Genesis 2:18–25; 1 Corinthians 6:15–20. Find as many reasons as you can from those bible passages why God created sex.

GROUP 2

Answer the question 'What are God's guidelines for a good marriage?' from these passages: Genesis 2:18–25; Matthew 19:4–6; 1 Corinthians 7:3–5.

Record your answers here with the appropriate bible references, and choose one of your group to report back to the other group.

MEMORY VERSE

1 Corinthians 6:19–20
'You do not belong to yourselves but to God; He bought you for a price.'

Key Example Two
Mark 11–16: The Gospel in One

INTRODUCTION

This example is taken from *Mark – Now teach the Gospel* published by CPAS.

Please read these notes before using it with your group.

Title

The title of this review session is important, so something like 'The Gospel in One' keeps it from sounding like a boring review.

Warm-up

Look out for ways of going back over the material which are fun. There are plenty of board games or TV games which can give us ideas. Here we suggest using the 'blockbusters' idea, but this is now getting a bit old hat. What's the latest TV quiz show? Could you use that, or at least take the idea and *adapt* it?

Mark One (Review One)

More on the 'fun', side, this suggests aiding memory by pointing our memorable things which happened on the teaching evening. This may have nothing at all to do with what you wanted to get across, but as a preliminary may well be very useful. Of course it would help this if at the end of each teaching session you made a note of, or keep, anything which jogs memories. You could ask one of your regular and reliable members to do this for you, and then ask them to bring their collection to this meeting.

Matching up the memory joggers, teaching aims and passages is a useful and fun way of helping to oil rusty memories. But remember that the purpose of a review session is to cement lessons learned in the hearts and minds of both you and your young people. It also encourages members to take action which they intended but never actually got round to.

Mark Two (Review Two)

Another useful (and slightly different) way of looking at a number of passages is to look for common themes. These may well come out as you look at the passages, so comment on them now.

Take action

God's reason for us reading the Bible is that we should change to become more like him. So we ask what changes have happened as a result of reading Mark, and what changes still need to happen. Reading the Bible is meant to change lives.

Leaders' hints

The review can also stimulate *us* to think back over how we have taught this, and how it could be improved. There is always room for improvement if our pride doesn't exclude the possibility.

THE SESSION

Aim to teach:

again, the lessons learned from Mark, but concentrating on chapters 11–16.

Aim that the group should:

be reminded and challenged regarding the application of the lessons from Mark 11–16.

Leading this session

This session could be very useful to you, as it will cement in your group's minds what they have learned, it will help them to see different passages in their context of the whole of Mark, it will help you to see how effective your teaching has been, and give you the opportunity of going over points which were unclear, problematical, or misunderstood, when you covered them the first time. So please don't omit this session!

Prepare, bearing in mind what has gone before in *your* group. And, as you lead the session, be ready to follow up specific areas which come to light, which need further clarification or re-statement.

Warm-up

Try one of these:

a) 'BLOCK-BUSTERS', with questions from Mark 11–16. It's easy to make your own 'Block-busters' board on a sheet of card, or on the OHP. Have suitable pens ready to fill in the squares as teams get the right answers.

Potential questions (to make it harder, ask for the chapter too!):

What C did Jesus ride into Jerusalem? (Colt – 11:7)

What H was the problem with the Pharisees and Herodians? (Hypocrisy – 12:15)

What D do the teachers of the law do to the widows' houses? (Devour – 12:40)

What C were the coins made of that the poor widow put into the temple treasury? (Copper – 12:42)

What S did the disciples marvel at in the temple? (Stones – 13:1)

What H did people cry when Jesus entered Jerusalem? (Hosannah – 11:9)

What G did Jesus go to after the resurrection? (Galilee – 14:28)

What W did Jesus want in the Garden of Gethsemane? (The will of God – 14:36)

What A was disputed by the chief priests, teachers of the law, and elders? (Authority – 11:28)

What P was where Jesus was mocked by the soldiers (Praetorium – 15:16)

What F was the tree that withered? (Fig – 11:20)

Which A joined Peter, James and John to ask Jesus when the temple would be destroyed? (Andrew – 13:3)

What L is what Jesus' body was wrapped in? (Linen – 15:46)

What S accompanied Mary and Mary to the tomb? (Salome – 16:1)

Which F knows the day and the hour? (The Father – 13:32)

What C were the crowd armed with when Jesus was arrested? (Clubs – 14:43)

What B did Jesus go to after the triumphal entry? (Bethany – 11:11)

What W must the disciples do when waiting for Jesus' return? (Watch – 13:37)

What A is where Joseph who buried Jesus, came from? (Arimathea – 15:43)

What F did the chief priests and teachers of the law feel towards Jesus? (Fear – 11:18)

What D did Jesus use to reveal the Pharisees' and Herodians' hypocrisy? (Denarius – 12:15)

What K does Pilate ask Jesus if He is? (King of the Jews – 15:2)

What U was the feast when the Passover lamb was sacrificed? (Unleavened bread – 14:12)

What P is the day before the Sabbath? (Preparation Day – 15:42)

b) 'RUDOLPH RACE': For a slightly larger group. Get teams of at least six to line up one behind the other. Deposit a large amount of lipstick onto the front nose of each group. The object of the exercise is to pass the lipstick down the line, and the winner is the one with the largest amount of lipstick on the nose of the back person in, say, one minute's time. At the end say that it is an excellent game for getting to know people better, and now we come to look back on what we have learned about Jesus, and how we have got to know Him better over the last year.

Introduce this session

by pointing out that this is an opportunity to review what you have learned in going through Mark's Gospel, and to clear up any misunderstandings and difficulties. We need to gain an overall picture of Mark, in order to understand the individual parts; that is the reason for this review session.

Mark's Gospel – Review 1

The aim of this exercise is to match up the main teaching points with one or two other memorable features of a particular evening, (e.g. the guest speaker, someone having a nose-bleed, news that someone had been given a job, etc) with the passage that was being studied. There is a "MEMORY JOGGERS" table to complete on GROUP EXTRA. Try one of the following ways, or, better still, think up your own!

a) Stay as one group, and have a 'Nostalgia Evening' as you look back over your studies in Mark (produce the visual aids you used, etc).

b) Write the ten *Aim to Teach* statements on pieces of paper, and devise ten memory joggers from your sessions putting these on separate pieces of paper, sticking them all up on the walls around the room (Post-it Notes are handy, and rarely leave a mark). Ask your group members to complete the GROUP EXTRA table as they walk around the room.

c) Write out the passages, teaching aims and memory joggers, all on separate cards, and deal these out to your group members, so that each member has one card. Then ask the members to mingle and to find the other two cards which link with theirs. As a result, the passage, main point and memory jogger will all link up correctly.

Having got your group members to remember what they learned, and how they learned it, you will now have the opportunity of recapping the important or misunderstood points as you go over their answers. Make sure you know the subject, are well prepared, and know what points you want to emphasise.

Take it in

Put your group into threes and ask them to consider carefully: 'Why did Mark write Mark 11–16?' Give them time and some possible alternatives, and ask them to choose (eg 'Because he knew Gospels have to have at least 16 chapters'. Or 'Because Jesus hadn't died at Chapter 10'. Or 'Because he had only answered one of his two questions'). As you handle the come-back, emphasise the overall structure of Mark, and the two main questions which Mark asks and answers, (i.e. 'Who was Jesus?', and 'Why did He come?').

Take a break

As an introduction to the theme search 'brainstorm' some of the main themes of Mark, and then, with these subjects, play 'Just a Minute'.

GROUP EXTRA

THINK
If Mark's Gospel had not survived, what would be missing from our picture of Jesus?

MEMORY JOGGERS

Passage	Main Point	Memory Joggers
Mark 11:1-26		
Mark 11:27-12:17		
Mark 12:18-44		
Mark 13:1-37		
Mark 14:1-25		
Mark 14:26-52		
Mark 14:53-72		
Mark 15:1-20		
Mark 15:21-39		
Mark 15:40-16:8		

"THE GOSPEL ACCORDING TO MARK?"

1 Jesus is ruler over the world
2 Jesus has the right to run our lives.
3 In one way or another, everyone rejects Jesus' right to run our lives.
4. God won't allow this to continue. If we reject Jesus, in the end He will reject us.
5. God sent Jesus to die for sin, in our place.
6. Jesus returned to life to show who He really is
7 We are called to stop being rebels, and live with Jesus as our King.

Minisaga

Mark's Gospel – Review 2

Try one of the following:

The Gospel in Mark

One of the aims of teaching the whole of Mark's Gospel is to teach our groups the Gospel by teaching Mark's Gospel. Ask your group to fill in the GROUP EXTRA 'The Gospel According to Mark?' table with references from Mark. You may need to help them here, so make sure you know the answers yourself beforehand!

Theme search

The following themes are strong in Mark 11–16: opposition and rejection, discipleship, service, the person of Jesus, the authority of Jesus, Jesus the teacher, fulfilment of prophecy. Take some, or all of these, and ask your group members to read Mark 11–16 (give them one chapter each), and find out what Mark has been saying about these themes. As they report back, write up a summary. Be sure they actually say what Mark has been saying.

Take it in

If your group likes writing, ask them to write a 50 word minisaga, which summarises Mark's Gospel. Then read out two or three, and perhaps write your own too, and explain why you have highlighted particular aspects.

Take action

Ask your group to jot down (privately) in the triangle shape on GROUP EXTRA, one thing which has changed in their own life since they have begun reading Mark. If anyone would like to share theirs, invite them to do so. You certainly should have something to say from *your* life, as leaders often learn a lot more than those they teach.

Second, ask the group to think of areas which still need working on, maybe as a group, or perhaps individually, and write these in the square. If there are any things which the group need to work on together, then talk about these, as a group.

Third, there may be something, as a result of today's session, which needs to be acted upon. Ask them to write this down in the circle, and to keep it private.

Equipment needed

- 'Block-busters' board
- Lipstick
- Copies of GROUP EXTRA
- Teaching Aims and Memory Jogger 'Post-Its' for the wall
- Visual aids which have been used before, to jog memories

Music suggestions

Jesus is King	LP 93 SHF 277
The Servant King	SHF 120 CFW 449

Leader's hints

Assessment – How has 'Mark NOW Teach the Gospel' gone? How well have you handled it? What lessons have you learned about teaching the Bible to your group?

Also, you may want to have a feed-back form on which you can ask your members which part they enjoyed most, and which part they enjoyed least, which part they learned most from, and which part they learned least from, what sort of teaching methods they prefer, etc. Group members cannot completely set the agenda of what we do, but we should listen carefully to their comments, as we plan for the future.

6

Seeing the Wood for the Trees – Coping with Difficult Passages

'*Why don't we just give up and do something else?*'

Daniel is a normally keen and supportive 16 year old, but on this particular Friday evening, it has all got a bit too much. His youth group have been looking at large chunks of Leviticus for three weeks now. Each time Dean, the youth leader, has attempted to stimulate their interest by having extended discussions on the shortcomings of the Old Testament sacrificial system. This week they are doing hands-on Bible study, with commentaries, Bible dictionaries, and different Bible versions open on the table in front of them, and they are attempting to find out all they can about the Old Testament feasts in Leviticus 23–27.

Seeing the title on the programme card, Emma and Rachel were diverted to McDonalds on their way over this evening, Pete has slipped out for a fag, and Danny claims his walkman helps him to concentrate. Jenny and Anne were too tired to come, and Jimmie developed some 'vital' homework that he just had to do.

Next week looks even better: 'Shock horror probe – the genealogy of 1 Chronicles 1–9'. They are already planning their excuses . . .

Should we even try to teach such parts of the Bible? Surely some bits are just so obscure and complicated that it's best to avoid them? And in other parts the relevant, useful, 'juicy' sections are so few and far between that it's just about impossible to teach them, especially if we are to do all the important things from chapter 3, like put it all in context.

Can't we just leave out these bits? – or at least rely on the church to teach them when our kids can cope with it?

These more obscure passages may be more useful where a group has a good number of slightly older Christians. The real core of our work is in teaching the gospels and epistles, and that is particularly important for groups which have mostly young Christians or non-Christians.

So don't feel guilty if you can't make these difficult passages work, or if you can't face doing them. But at the same time I want to encourage you to give it a go. With care, it's perfectly possible to bring these passages to life. Such passages shouldn't be the staple diet of the group: more an occasional feast, like Christmas lunch.

Long passages – the big con job

Are you as scared of long and difficult passages as I am? We end up thinking some of the following:

- '*I can't understand it, so I can't teach it.*'
  But with a bit of hard work and the help of study aids and other people, the dawn of understanding *is* possible. Ask your vicar/minister/pastor.

- '*Our young people couldn't understand it, so we won't bother.*'
  But don't underestimate them. If you can understand it, there is a pretty good chance they'll grasp it too.

- '*There's far too much to read in one evening.*'
  Well normally, yes, but there are ways and means, as we shall see.

- '*There's nothing worth teaching there anyway.*'
  Many people say that before they've looked!

- '*They're usually from the Old Testament, and our young people just don't like the Old Testament.*'
  Where did they get that idea from? It may be because you don't like the Old Testament. And the reason for that *may* be that you haven't spent much time with the Old Testament. Try getting to grips with an Old Testament book, or just reading through the Old Testament in a year.

- '*There are no good resources to help me teach this.*'
  There are good straightforward commentaries (see Special One) and study aids. They don't give you the session on a plate, but they are a great help in the cooking.

- '*No-one in our youth group is interested in all this stuff.*'
  Try it and see, and be enthusiastic. Their interest depends on yours. Your enthusiasm is infectious.

- '*It sounds too much like hard work.*'
  It *is* hard work. But we want to provide a healthy and balanced diet. And within that, some bits are more indigestible than others and take longer to prepare. Don't duck this just because it's harder work than other sessions.

Difficult passages – useful but neglected

Just supposing that we *can* cope with long or difficult passages, why should we even try?

- **There's a reason.** The divine author has a reason for including each part of Scripture. That reason may be well hidden. It may be more relevant for others than for us. But there is one, and it means that each part of the Bible has a point, and is worth teaching. So don't dismiss certain passages because they are difficult to understand. To dismiss Einstein's discoveries because he is 'too difficult' would only reveal our ignorance and foolishness. To dismiss Leviticus may have the same effect.

- **It's a revelation.** Hard work on some of these longer and more difficult passages reveals hidden gems. Diligence pays off.
  I decided one day that there must be something worthwhile in those dreadfully long and boring genealogies of 1 Chronicles 1–9, so I took a deep breath and got stuck in with a commentary. And I found that there is some stunning stuff in there.
  It is actually a series of family trees, with selective comments, giving invaluable background to why the Chronicler wrote 1 and 2 Chronicles. He is writing to the people of Israel when they

are going through an identity crisis, and the family trees give vital roots and information which helped the people of Israel answer the question, 'Who are we?'

● **It's a possibility.** When did you last do Ezekiel or 2 Kings with your youth group? Be broad. It is possible.

Special One

Is that really in the Bible?
Eight Important Passages We Leave Out

None of these are particularly easy passages, but try to cover them, or passages like these, from time to time with your group.

1 1 Chronicles 1–9

This long genealogy looks impossible to read, let alone study. It's probably best not to ask your group to read it out loud, but it contains important insights. I found the 'Bible Speaks Today' commentary on 1 and 2 Chronicles (IVP) very helpful.

2 John 15–17

Do you think you understand John? Or like me are you a bit scared of it? Chapters 15–17 contain some very important teaching. Maybe get your minister to come and explain them to your group, or to talk to you about it so you can explain it to your group.

3 Isaiah

The whole book is too long for a short series. We could select references to Jesus, but that would be to ignore the historical setting of the book. So we should also look at what Isaiah is saying to the Jews of his day. One session on the biography of Isaiah would be useful for this, as would time spent on impending judgement in Isaiah 8–10, 22–24, 34, and another session on hope in Isaiah 27, 35, 37, 40, 47, 49, 54.

4 Leviticus

Read it through once, and the idea of teaching it sounds horrific. But with the idea in the back of our minds that it's all about holiness, we could, for example, tackle the five types of offering in chapters 1–7, the work of the priests in chapters 8–10, and moral laws in chapters 18–20, stressing why they are there, and what, if any, relevance they have for us now. A good Old Testament introduction would be invaluable here!

5 Matthew 1:1–17

This is not so difficult as regards length, but it still seems pretty obscure. Try looking at why Matthew starts his gospel with a genealogy, and pick out some of the key people (eg Abraham, David, Hezekiah). Look at the women who appear in it.

6 Revelation

This is every young person's favourite book, and every youth leader's nightmare. The letters to the seven churches in Revelation 1–3 are fine, but after that the confusion begins. But Revelation is best done in larger chunks, because to concentrate on every detail only multiplies confusion.

Use a good commentary – again the Bible Speaks Today on Revelation (IVP) is very useful. Maybe do three sessions on the Seven Seals (chapters 6–7), the Seven Trumpets (chapters 8–11) and the Seven Bowls (chapters 15–16). Your young people may find it helpful to be told that we don't understand all the detail, but we can grasp the general picture – and that's what Revelation is, a picture.

7 Ezekiel

Ezekiel was a bizarre individual with a powerful message. A biographical evening on Ezekiel himself would be a good start, and then an evening on 'the message'. Use a good commentary and introduction to teach your group what the book *as a whole* is about, with examples from specific passages. 'Divine judgement' is the main thrust, and it has clear application today to those without God. With this as a background, in the weeks that follow look at specific passages such as Ezekiel 12, 16, 33, 37.

8 Song of Songs

Try not to be embarrassed when teaching this! Tackle it all at one go, and teach your young people, quite simply, the beauty of love. If you want a good starter for the following week's evening on relationships and marriage, look no further.

Reading long and difficult passages

Young people's concentration span is short at the best of times, and there are certain activities which make it worse. Reading the Bible out loud is one of them. Young people can just about cope with reading a parable, or half a chapter from Philippians, but ninety-seven verses from Numbers is one sure way of extinguishing any flickering flame of interest right at the start of a teaching evening.

Here are some ideas to help:

- **Advance warning.** Tell the group beforehand that you will be doing this so they'll know what to expect. It will also make life easier, if they have read the passage before they come.

- **Speciality.** Some people are real specialists at reading the Bible aloud. Somehow when they read the Bible, it comes alive. If you've got someone like that in your church, ask them along to read the passage to your group next week.

- **Breakdown.** Divide the passage into bite-sized chunks. For instance, take a chapter at a time with a song or an activity in between. Some groups have managed to read a whole Bible book at a sitting using this method. Or you could take a whole gospel, stopping half way through for chips.

- **Involvement.** Be careful here of non-readers, but aim to use the fact that involvement heightens interest. Use your imagination here. Don't just 'read round', but ask group members to take different parts and then swop these around at each chapter break, arranging this in advance. Or ask your group to act it out, or read it, all together.

- **Audio.** There is an increasing number of cassettes available of the Bible being read – and being read well. It would make a good change to use one. If appropriate, have it as a bedtime story, with subdued lighting and Bibles closed. But know your group first: this could end up in chaos!

- **Story.** Tell the story of the chapters you are covering, picking out key verses from the passage to illustrate as you go through (see Key Example 2).

- **Precis.** Pick out certain shorter sections of the passage which tell the account but leave out the detail. Ask group members to read these as in Key Example 2. You may want to try a combination of story and precis.

- **Highlight.** Highlight some aspect such as the personality of a Bible character. Arrange to have the relevant verses read out. But put this in the context of the rest of the passage, and for this you may need some precis as well. It may be handy to physically highlight the passage for each of your group members either by typing it out or copying it, and then using a highlight pen.

- **Versions.** Do try and make sure people have all the same version so that they can follow more easily.

- **Variety.** Mix up a number of these methods in one evening, and vary the use of them from week to week.

Special Two
Long and Difficult Passages:
The Youth Leader's Toolbox

The following eight items will be useful to any youth leader who wants to teach any of these long passages to his or her group.

1 An introduction to the books of the Bible

The excellent *'Bible from Scratch'* by Simon Jenkins (Lion), is invaluable for us and can be given to group members. Also try the NIV Study Bible which has a brief introduction and commentary to each book, or one of the introductions published by Lion or IVP. Look for books which give the main points and the aim of the Bible book in short sharp sections.

2 Ability to read the Bible like a book

We often read the Bible as if every word and punctuation mark is of vital significance. It may well be, but when looking at long passages it's more useful at first to read the Bible like an ordinary book. Read large chunks at a sitting. Read through the long passage as if it were a novel. Then when you've got the whole thing under your belt, come back and study it.

3 Courage

This is the ability not to shy away from the more difficult passages and the guts to take them on, confident that it is possible to teach them well to your group.

4 A modern, readable version

Versions which are not in today's language hinder most young people's understanding. It's also helpful if everyone can have their own Bible and in the same version. Encourage them to bring their own, and to ask for a particular version for birthday or Christmas. Have a few spares available, but stress that these are only for emergencies. Don't let the group rely on them.

5 Notebook and pen

Jot down findings as you read through. Make a note of verses to come back to, and any thoughts about themes, possible teaching points or presentation methods.

6 A comfy armchair

This is for sitting in when reading the long passage. Make yourself comfortable, and make sure there's plenty of time to read it again.

7 Excitement

Don't think it's going to be boring and tedious even before you start. Instead be expectant, enthusiastic, and excited about the job in hand. And of course, do take time to pray carefully about it first.

8 Time

Longer passages do take a long time to prepare. Try to plan ahead, and block out the extra time that will be necessary. Share the workload with other leaders.

Key Example 1
Exodus Chapters 2–4
'Man of the Moment'

INTRODUCTION

Before you use this with your group, note the following:

Teaching point

Despite there being three chapters to read, there is one unifying thought and therefore one main teaching point. This is that God usually works on earth by working through people. There are many other points that could be taught, but it's far more effective to have a narrow sharpened aim.

Take off

The session notes suggest that we tell our young people what we are wanting to communicate at the start. It helps if *we* know what we're trying to say. It helps if they know too.

First leg

1. Inducements to read the whole of the three chapters are one way of getting concentration (unless they're concentrating on the toffees or the coffee!).

2. This uses members' investigation as they scan through chapters 2–4, but especially chapter 2, in search of facts about Moses. This detective work is useful for members' integration and involvement in the meeting, but make sure they are finding 'What the Bible is actually saying'. Check this in the comeback, and know the material yourself.

In flight entertainment

Long passages can appear more boring than others, so the need for lighter sections is highlighted. Note through, that this is still firmly tied in to the main thrust of the meeting – Moses the man who God works through.

Second leg

Again uses the group involvement in the investigation of Moses' qualifications and disqualifications. Note that splitting the group up can be done to save time as well as to incorporate variety.

Touch down

Young people often feel that long passages are irrelevant, so the earthing of such passages is important. The key to this is successfully working out what the long passage means, and hence the importance of both First Leg and Second Leg, but especially in this instance the Second leg. But it also needs to be earthed and the implications realized, so Touch Down is important too. It's introduced by recapping the meaning of the passage from First Leg and Second Leg, and then made personal by asking questions about how God wants to work through *me*.

The picking of favourite verses without saying why and what I'm going to do about it is a dangerous occupation If it's earthed, though, it can be kept relevant to the overall thrust of the passage.

THE SESSION

Teaching point

That God normally works through people despite their inadequacies.

Group aim

That they should see that God will use them, and begin to see how he can overcome their inadequacies.

Teaching Long and Difficult Passages

There are a number of things to mention here for our preparation, and then several ideas about taking the session.

(a) In Preparation

1. *Know your stuff*

Teaching is always hampered if we're unsure of the subject, and this is particularly common when looking at long passages or other difficult parts of the Bible.

For looking at the Old Testament it would be good to have read an Old Testament background such as John Drane's *Introducing the Old Testament* or *The Old Testament Story*, both published by Lion, and an introduction to the particular book. The excellent *Bible from Scratch* by Simon Jenkins (Lion) would be a worthwhile investment here, both for you, and to give to group members.

2. *Really get into the passage*

It will require extra work in preparation, but if we are on top of the passage, that will be a great help. And a valuable side effect of this is:

3. *Enthusiasm*

Every (yes, every) part of the Bible can be exciting if we have worked on it, know it, and have let God speak to us through it. Excitement is infectious, so if we are excited by a passage, so will our groups be.

But we're often so busy that there is no time to dwell on the passage and let it get inside us and excite us. Just that little bit extra time in preparation could be well worthwhile.

4. *Hard work*

Long passages therefore need even more hard work than usual. If you're a full-timer you may have the time for that. But if you're married with a family and a demanding job, it may be just too much – or at least too much to tackle a long passage more than very occasionally. If that's you, you're not a failure. You're just taking your other responsibilities seriously.

(b) In Practice

You are confronted by four chapters of the history of Israel, and forty minutes with your young people to try to teach them something worthwhile from this. It's a bit like being given an enormous loaf of bread and being told to feed it to others. Some would select certain parts and so cut off the crust and give out the dough. Others would aim to eat it systematically, one part at a time. A few would compress it to make eating easier. Whatever method, we need to make the loaf, and the passage, manageable. Both we and our members need to be able to approach the task thinking 'I can cope with this'. How?

1. Just the usual principles

All the usual points about finding the dominant or key thought, the main teaching point, still apply. There is an argument for saying that no matter how long a passage is, it's still possible to find one key thought, one main point to teach. Even the whole Bible could be summed up in something like 'God creating a people for Himself'.

So still take Chapter 3 seriously, and work out your teaching point. What is the passage saying? Our main task is still the same. The two main differences with handling long passages are the amount of preparation we have to do to be on top of it, and what methods we use to keep the members' attention when we read and teach it.

2. Talk, an ordinary talk

This is often the easiest way, and may be the best on many occasions. Here we can focus in on key points, and if your group has been used to active learning, it will make a good change. Use a talk to give a bird's-eye view of the passage, pointing out the key features without the accompanying danger of utter confusion which group work sometimes entails.

3. Divide

That is, divide the passage up between the group members and ask them to look out for particular aspects. You could use the same question about all the different parts of this evening's passage. Or use a different exercise or different questions for different chunks of the passage on view. This is breaking it down into mouth-sized chunks.

It is important to give group members a clear understanding of the parts of the passage which they haven't tackled. They will get a good grasp of the part which they've investigated, but may well not really understand the parts which they haven't tackled unless we make it absolutely clear to them.

4. Prune – down to the bare minimum

You may decide to focus on one aspect, and therefore just look at a few verses, while putting them in the context of the whole passage. Or look for one passage or a few verses which effectively summarize the whole thing. The latter may not be possible, and the former may not be desirable. We are after all trying to look at the whole of a long and possibly difficult passage. But it was worth a thought anyway.

5. Precis

Give a summary of what the passage is saying. Try this visually. A picture, however poor, conveys a *lot* of information easily. Or re-tell the story in your own words, picking out key parts. Or ask the group to produce a 'mini-saga' to summarize the passage in no more than 25 or perhaps 50 words. If you do this yourself in the preparation, it's a very good discipline, and also shows whether it is possible or not.

6. *Highlight*

Copy the passage or have it typed out, perhaps by a group member, and then highlight key verses. This will help members to see the thread of the story and/or get hold of the main points more easily.

7. *Members' Investigation*

This makes the evening like detective work, with members having to find out certain information from the passage. Ask them to search through for clues to someone's character – God's, perhaps. Ask them to look for common threads in the passage.

With an older and smaller group, it's possible to employ the hands-on method, where you sit around a table with different versions, a concordance, cross references, simple commentaries, Bible atlases, Bible dictionaries and introductions and the like, and work out together what the passage is about. With your enthusiasm and guidance, this works very well. Maybe this is something to save to a midweek meeting for the keener and/or older ones.

[Presentation idea: summary of above 7 points in a box.]

And then with these ideas in mind, it is perfectly possible to use, after adaptation, many of the methods from Chapter 5. The knack in coping with long passages is to concentrate the information into small enough chunks so that people can get hold of it. Once that is done, the variety of methods outlined in Chapter 5 can be applied.

For examples of how it is possible to handle long passages, see the Key Examples at the end of the Chapter.

Pre-flight checks

It's important in this session for people to grasp what Moses was like. This is the main aim of 'First Leg'. But bear in mind that you really need to get through to 'Second Leg' which contains the main teaching point of the session. So remember this as you prepare, and as you lead. Prune material from the first half so you have time to concentrate on the more important issues in the second half. Our role is not just to teach about Moses, but also to see the relevance of this for us today.

Check in

Try one of these ice-breakers:

- **Baby match up.** Ask people to bring baby photographs of themselves. Put them up on a board and get people to match the photos with the group members.

- **Mix and match.** Ask members to write one obscure fact about themselves on a piece of paper, throw these into a bin, and then draw them out one at a time and try to match these up with the individuals present. Ask that facts from their distant past should be given.

After both or either of these activities explain that you're looking at Moses, and in particular at the earlier years of his life.

Take-off

Explain to your group that you are going to see how God works on earth. He normally does this by working through people. Here we have an example of a great thing which God wanted to do, and he accomplishes it by using a person: Moses. Moses wouldn't be our automatic choice, but he was God's 'man of the moment'. First we will see a little background to Moses (First Leg) and then we begin to see how God works out his plans for Israel through Moses (Second Leg).

First leg

Ask your group to complete the Moses fact file on the Group Extra page. Although this involves reading the whole of chapters 2–4, most of the information is in chapter 2. So you could ask your group to read chapter 2 only, and then fill in the rest from the preparation which you have done. Or else divide your group up into three and give each group one chapter to examine.

It is perfectly possible to read chapters 2–4 in one sitting – it doesn't take nearly as long as you think and the story is very fast moving with a lot of variety. If your group don't have a great concentration span, then try offering them inducements of, say, passing round a box of toffees after each chapter or by stopping for coffee once they've reached the end of chapter 4.

Once the group have filled in their Moses fact file, you will need to highlight the 'Man of the moment' element here and show how God is in control right from the start of Moses' life. God has a job for Moses to do, and we can see God's sovereignty in this right from the beginning.

Inflight entertainment

'Disqualified'

Tell your group that each individual within the group has been put forward as the next mayor/vicar/prime minister/headmaster etc (choose the most appropriate!), and they have to write down on a slip of paper the following:

● What the job is.
● Why they couldn't *possibly* do it, thinking of all possible reasons.
In pairs or in small groups give their slip to someone else who has three minutes to argue why they *could* do it. They should then give the person who they are encouraging their arguments for why they should take on the job, then finish this particular section by tearing up the original slips of paper.

This leads on to second leg, where we see what Moses' excuses were, and how God dealt with them.

'Encourager'

You could play this right at the beginning of the session, or here as an introduction to the second leg if you haven't already done a lot of detailed work on Moses' character. So before you've actually looked at Moses' character in depth, ask your group to do a problem-solving exercise. Say that you want Chris (or any other suitably named individual) to be the next prime minister, but he/she is tongue-tied, shy, unsure about the idea, has no background in politics, and doesn't want to do it. He/she does have a good education, a good character, but generally seems uninterested in the job.

Ask your group to think up what they would say to Chris to encourage them to take on the job. You may ask them to write a letter to this person. Then ask your group members to present their ideas to the rest of the group. You can either do this by volunteers reading out their contributions, or ask them to swap letters with their neighbours, then getting their neighbours to read it out if the one they've been given is better than the one they wrote in the first place.

Second leg

Ask your group to work through Exodus 2–4 again and pull out all the qualifications and disqualifications that Moses has for the job of leading the people of Israel. Collage these onto a large sheet of paper or OHP with two columns (qualifications/disqualifications). If you're running short of time you could split your group into three and ask them to shout our their findings.

Once you have a list in both columns, ask your group if they were looking for someone for the job of leading Israel, would they actually employ Moses? Then you may like to make the point that, apart from being a murderer, the two columns could very easily describe us.

Point out that Moses doesn't seem to be the best possible choice for the task in hand. Now the important point is to ask how God answered this problem.

Show your group that the main way God responded to Moses was to say that he (God) had made his decision, and that was all that was necessary because God would equip Moses for the task he wanted him to do.

Also note the following:

- It is God's work rather than Moses' work (3:7–8) and Moses is used as God's instrument (3:10).
- Because of Moses' timidity, God gives him signs that he is with Moses (3:12, 4:1–9).
- God instructs Moses to work through the elders of Israel (3:16–18). This is a way of enlisting the support of the leadership of the people of Israel.
- God gave Moses a spokesman – his brother Aaron (4:13–15).

One final important thing to draw out is that Moses' response was to *obey*. 4:18–31 gives several examples of Moses doing precisely what God had commanded (note especially, 4:18, 27, 29–31).

Touch down

Recap first leg and second leg and re-emphasise that this is about God working through people, who are often reluctant and 'disqualified'.

Now drum the point home and apply it:

1 Ask your group members individually to answer these three questions:
   a) What does God want *me* to do as a result of this passage?
   b) What are my underlying objections to this?
   c) How does God answer these?
(You may need to give some help in answering a) by giving general teaching about God wanting us all to become more like him).

2 Ask group members to pick out a favourite verse from Exodus 2–4 and then to work out what they're going to *do* about it. Turn to a friend (or do this as a whole group) and share not only their favourite verse, but also *why*, and *what* this means they have to do this coming week.

Group Extra – Moses Fact File

Mother

Father

Brothers and sisters

Early childhood

Education

Character

Wife

Children

Career outline

Key Example 2
Exodus 12–14 'Memory Lane'

INTRODUCTION

Note the following:

1 Despite having to tackle three chapters, there is still one main theme which binds it all together, and therefore one main teaching point – the theme being that of our need to remember the sovereign rule of God.

2 This teaching point isn't as obvious as it could be. Our young people need to know the *events* of the Old Testament, but also the meaning of them today. We can no longer assume that they know about the Passover, Exodus and crossing the Red Sea. We also need to teach carefully the point about the need to remember the great acts of God in history.

3 The check-in games are there to reinforce the need to remember. Game number 2 may be useful to think back over last week's meeting. It will help your members remember what was learned then, and will be helpful for you to see what they did actually remember.

4 Reading the long passage: if you try 2, then make sure you give a brief introduction, and perhaps a running commentary. These brief passages don't just run one into the other.

5 First leg: the group does a lot of work by looking at separate chapters. If you do this, make sure they understand the place of *their* chapter in the whole. It's easy to get immersed in detail and fail to see the whole picture.

6 First leg – artistic work. This can be a very useful way of communicating a lot of information quickly, even if the drawings are hopeless.

7 In flight entertainment. The memory joggers are supposed to get the group to understand the value of the Passover and the Feast of Unleavened Bread. Why not make some unleavened bread? Make sure you use memory joggers that actually work! If you use ones that fail, the whole point of the exercise is ruined.

8 The second leg. This involves looking at large chunks again, but getting the group members to take on this investigation themselves. Here again the key to successful communication is that the *others* in the group realize and understand what each of the other groups has been studying, so good handling of feedback is vital.

9 Touchdown. This is vital, so don't miss it. Practical memory tips can be useful for us all, so we mustn't exclude ourselves from the application of ideas.

THE SESSION

Teaching point

The need to *remember* the sovereign rule of God.

Group aim

To take practical steps to remember what God has done for them.

Pre-flight checks

It would be very easy to get carried away here and just concentrate on the remarkable events of the Exodus and the crossing of the Red Sea. However we must rely on the Bible not only to give us the facts of history, but also to yield an interpretation.

The apparently mundane chapter 13, sandwiched between the staggering events of chapter 12 (the Passover and Exodus) and chapter 14 (crossing the Red Sea) is in fact very important. That's because it is here that the people of Israel are told of the need to *remember* what has happened (and are given aids to do this). The great acts of God are not just to be left in history, but are to be actively remembered.

In the New Testament, we see the same principle in operation. Christianity is firmly based on the great acts of God in history (namely Jesus' death and resurrection), and our response is to remember these, and then act on them.

Check in

Try one of these memory games:

- **Pelmanism.** In this memory card game, a set of cards are placed face down, and players have to pick out pairs by taking it in turns to turn over two cards, and then placing them face down again if they aren't pairs. Players with most pairs win.

    A variation is to take a roll of film of your group the week before, and, have it developed with an extra set of prints, and then play pelmanism with the photos. For extra fun, you could say that they can keep the pairs they collect, and see which ones are the most popular! You may want to guard against over-competitiveness by giving a prize to the player with the least pairs.

- **Last week.** Ask members to jot down (or shout out for you to collate on the OHP/wallsheet), as much as they can remember of last week's meeting. Don't forget the teaching point, but also remember who wore what, who arrived late, what you prayed for, who wasn't there, what biscuits you had, and any other memorable points about the meeting.

Takeoff

Explain to your group that although you are going to be looking at three of the most memorable events of the Old Testament (the Passover, Exodus, and Crossing of the Red Sea), that the main thing that we are going to be remembering is the need to <u>actually</u> remember these. God wants us to remember what He has done, and helps us to do this.

First leg

First, read the passage. Since it's long, you may want to employ one of these methods:

- **In parts.** This will take some time, so watch the clock, but if you're prepared it can be very valuable. When you prepare, read the passage carefully and decide how many readers you'll need. And also make sure that you've got enough copies of the same version of the Bible.

- **Pick out key passages.** Just read these and so give your members an overview of the whole section. You could type these out to form a precis on one sheet of paper, and then have it copied for everyone in the group, but whatever you do make sure that you read the whole passage several times yourself. If you use this

method, make sure you include at least the following passages:
12:5, 12–15, 17–19, 29–31, 37–39
13:7–9, 14–16
14:4–9, 13–14, 21–28, 31

- **Tell the story.** Tell the account in your own words but quote key verses from the passage in order to substantiate what you say.

  Suggested key verses would be:
  12:12, 14, 15, 17, 29
  13:14
  14:4, 13–14, 21, 22, 26, 28, 31

In the first teaching segment, concentrate on the great acts which God did for the people of Israel. You will need to ask 'What actually happened?', and draw out the fact that God is in control.

Divide your group into three, and ask the first third to look at the Passover and the Feast of Unleavened Bread (12:1–30), the second third to look at the Exodus (12:31–42), and the final third to look at the Crossing of the Red Sea (14:1–31). Ask all groups to look at these questions:

- What did God do? (they may like to search for verbs which underline what God did).
- What did the people have to do?
- Why did a) God, and b) the people, act in this way?

Ask each group to draw up a telemessage of no more than twenty-five words to summarise their findings. If you have two or more groups covering each area (Passover and Unleavened Bread/ Exodus/ Red Sea), then ask the scribe from each group to go to another one and read out their telemessages. Then if the receiving group thinks that the message they've been read is better than the one they wrote, get the scribe to read it out to the whole group.

You will need to have prepared carefully, so that you can fill in and stress the points which are either not made by group members, or which are made poorly. Make sure at the end of this session that everyone has a good idea not only of *what* happened, but *why* it happened.

For the more artistic, after (or instead of), the telemessages, ask groups or individuals to draw a quick sketch to summarise their findings. It should include not only *what* happened but also the *reasons* for it. (The reasons will be harder to portray than the facts, so don't have over-high expectations!)

As before, groups swap scribes/artists and they can explain the picture to the new group. When a group comes across a better picture than theirs this could be shown to all the members present.

Inflight entertainment

- **Memory Joggers.** Collect about 15–20 different small items and keep them concealed in a bag. Equip members with pens/paper, and then explain what you are going to do. Take each item out of the bag, show it briefly to the group, and place it in another bag, so the members have a brief glimpse of each item in turn. When all the items have been shown, allow members sixty seconds to write down as many as they can remember.

  Then jog their memories. Do this by
  a) giving them a list of the first letters of each item
  b) showing them briefly a photo of the items (you'll have to be organised, but if you've taken photos for the check-in, you could use the same film).
  c) tell them quickly a list of things they could *do* with the items
  d) think up your own way of jogging their memories!

Make sure you make the point that for the people of Israel, these events were very important, but they also had to remember them, so God gave them memory joggers. He does that too in the New Testament; so, for instance, the Communion Service helps us to remember the great things God has done for us in Jesus death.

Second leg

In this segment, concentrate on the *remembering* aspect of these passages. Ask your group to scan through Exodus 12–14 and search out all references to the people of Israel having to remember what God was doing. You could divide up your group and give each part a section of the passage to look at. Perhaps give each group a piece of OHP acetate (if you're using one) and pen, or a piece of paper and marker pen on which to write out relevant verses. Make sure they don't write out huge chunks – there's no need to.

Alternatively, write out a summary yourself, and show this to the group once they've done their work.

Whichever method you use, the main verses you will want to point out are: 12:14, 17, 24–27, 47, and 13:5, 6, 9, 10, 14.

Outline reasons why we forget and therefore why we need to make a conscious effort to remember what God has done for us. Then cover ways which you have found to be good in helping *you* to remember what God has done.

Ask your group members to brainstorm how they remember things. Do this on to the OHP/wallchart. Have a few ideas up your sleeve (I remember by writing it down, telling someone else, repeating it ten times, tying a knot in my handkerchief, asking someone to remind me, etc). Ask them to select two which they could use to help them not to forget what God has done for them.

Touchdown

Ask the group to write down or tell the person sitting next to them what Christians have to remember. You may need to remind them that it's the Gospel which Christians have to remember – the death of Jesus Christ for our sin and his resurrection from the dead.

Then ask them to select one way to help them remember this from the list drawn up at the end of the second leg. Write that down too.

Give the group (and yourself) one minute to pray about being better at remembering what God has done for us.

7

The Long Lost Art of
Teaching Christian Doctrine

It's Sunday evening again at St Chad's, and there's a certain amount of tension between the leaders of the church youth group. The members have noticed it too, and they are also getting very bored. The problem is that at the last leaders' meeting, well over four months ago now, Stephen, who tends to think he is related to John Calvin, had the 'bright' idea that the group should have some sessions on Christian doctrine. The other leaders reluctantly agreed, and are now regretting it. Stephen took on the whole series of six, and they are now on number four. So far he has ploughed through the doctrine of Christ – His Person, His Work and His Reign. Now he is going on to the doctrine of Man, and today he has promised to give a riveting exposé of total depravity. The other leaders aren't so convinced . . .

For many churches and youth groups, doctrine has gone out of fashion.

That's presumably why whenever you mention the word 'doctrine', 95% of people switch off. Like football supporters, doctrine has made a bad name for itself. Or to be more precise, *we* have earned doctrine a bad name by the way we have talked about it and handled it. But please read on; it's an important subject. Doctrine is rather like vitamins. They are essential for a healthy diet. We eat them with every meal, but the occasional vitamin supplement also does us a lot of good.

Many Christian young people today have only a vague grasp of the foundations of their Christian faith. One reason for that is our failure to teach them doctrine

This has two important side effects.

- *Those without a clear grasp of their faith are likely to be blown off course.* Paul warns of this in Ephesians 4:14, where the Christians in Ephesus are encouraged to grow up by using the gifts of the church so that they may have a firmer grasp of what they believe: 'Then we will no longer be infants, tossed back and forth by the waves, and blown here and there by every wind of teaching and by the cunning craftiness of men in their deceitful scheming.'

- *Those with a shallow faith are more likely to give up.* Just as a tree with poor roots is a likely candidate for uprooting in a storm, so is a poorly equipped Christian when times get tough. Teaching Christian doctrine is a good way of providing a sound understanding of our faith.

But what *is* Christian doctrine anyway? It has been called simply 'a description of what Christians believe about God and his relations with the world'. Doctrine gives a structure into which we can fit further knowledge about God as we learn this from the Bible.

Some people still insist that doctrine is very tedious. But if you stop and think for just one moment about what God has done for us, how could that *possibly* be boring?

In today's church we are better at some things than others – we're not bad at worship; sometimes we're quite good at getting involved in the community; we can be pretty useful at working up a very good atmosphere in our groups; and some people are even good at teaching young people the Bible. But teaching Christian doctrine is a weak point. '. . .this dismissal of doctrines, is, in my judgement, nothing short of a recipe for disaster'. Bruce Milne, *Know The Truth*.

Christian doctrine – neglected but important

There are some things which we can afford to neglect. I regularly neglect to cut the grass in our back garden. It doesn't look very nice, but I can get away with neglecting it.

But can our youth groups get away with neglecting Christian doctrine?

Short run or long run?

In the short run, yes, they can get away with it. In the long run, they can't. In the short run, our young people will have a somewhat shallow happy-go-lucky faith, but they still come along, and even bring their friends. They aren't much good at telling right from wrong or saying what exactly it is that they believe, but they are keen, and do seem to be growing as Christians.

But in the long run, that shallow Christianity is a weak Christianity, unable to discern wisdom from folly, truth from falsehood, tossed around by every new theological idea, vague as to the biblical demands on Christians, and unable to clearly put into words what they believe.

Mindless wandering?

Christianity is about using our minds. 'Jesus replied: "Love the Lord your God with all your heart, and with all your soul, and with all your mind." (Matthew 22:37). We *all* have minds. We can *all* think to some degree or another, and God wants everyone to apply their minds to their faith.

This does not mean, 'be academic'. It *does* mean, however, that we need to think about what we believe. But I hear you say: 'I'm no theologian'. Yes you are! If you are a Christian, you *are* a theologian. That's because theology is literally, 'the study of God'.

Special One

Doctrine – Where Would We Be Without It?

Tackling Christian doctrine is a bit like taking a vitamin supplement. It's also a bit like air – we only tend to notice it when there is a lot of it around and it's windy, or when there isn't enough. Doctrine gives us:

- *Depth in the understanding of our faith.*
  Without it, we simply wouldn't know what it was that we believed, and would find it hard to think more deeply about our faith.

- *A link between the Gospel and our lifestyle.*
  If we don't understand what we believe, it's harder to work out the implications that this has for the way we live.

- *A defence against heresy.*
  If we are not sure what is right, how can we tell what's dubious and what's wrong?

- *A structure to help us understand less well known passages of the Bible.*
  Doctrine gives a framework within which to understand new passages of the Bible. So when we are exploring a new area of the Bible, we have a framework to help us understand what it is about.

- *Clarity in our understanding.*
  This structure helps us to think more clearly about what we do believe and what we don't believe.

- *A basis for clear communication.*
  Without doctrine it is far more difficult to communicate our faith both with other Christians (so that we can work together) and with non-Christians, (so that we can tell them what we believe).

Christian doctrine – why do it?

What are the advantages of studying Christian doctrine?

It's Biblical

- Doctrine is clearly important in the Bible, and especially in the later letters of the New Testament, where beliefs are being sorted out in the early church, and Paul constantly reminds Timothy of the importance of teaching sound doctrine.

> You must teach what is in accord with sound doctrine.
> (Titus 2:1).

- There is the excitement of finding out God's mind on the subject, and seeing that the Bible has one mind on these matters – it's a unity rather than a compendium of conflicting ideas.

It's relevant

That's because it relates directly to the problems we face in everyday life. Doctrine equips us to live our Christian lives better, because what we believe affects how we live. So, for example, if you believe that a low fat diet will reduce your cholesterol, you will cut down on the fried eggs for breakfast.

> If correct doctrine does not lead to holy, loving, mature lives, something has gone terribly wrong. (Bruce Milne, *Know the Truth*).

More than that, if we are clear about what we believe (ie our doctrine is clear), then it will be easier to explain it to others. Clear doctrine helps evangelism.

It's important

The New Testament is full of warnings about false teachers.

'Anyone who breaks one of the least of these commandments and teaches others to do the same will be called the least in the Kingdom of Heaven, but whoever practises and teaches these commands will be called great in the kingdom of heaven' (Matthew 5:19).

'They worship me in vain, their teachings are but rules taught by men' (Matthew 15:9).

'They want to be teachers of the law, but they do not know what they are talking about or what they so confidently affirm' (1 Timothy 1:7).

'The Spirit clearly says that in later times some will abandon the faith and follow deceiving spirits and things taught by demons' (1 Timothy 4:1).

'If anyone teaches false doctrines and does not agree to the sound instruction of our Lord Jesus Christ and to godly teaching, he is conceited and understands nothing' (1 Timothy 6:3–4).

'The time will come when men will not put up with sound doctrine. Instead, to suit their own desires, they will gather around them a great number of teachers to say what their itching ears want to hear' (1 Timothy 4:3).

'They must be silenced, because they are ruining whole households by teaching things they ought not to teach – and that for the sake of dishonest gain' (Titus 1:11).

'But there were also false prophets among the people, just as there will be false teachers among you. They will secretly introduce destructive heresies, even denying the sovereign Lord who bought them – bringing swift destruction on themselves' (2 Peter 2:1)

With no sound basis for what we believe, there is no reliable method of knowing whether what we are hearing or reading is right or wrong. Teaching our groups doctrine will help to give this sound basis.

It's educational

- It's a good way of doing our job. Teaching doctrine is a very good way of presenting refined and defined truth which young people can latch on to easily.

- Teaching doctrine will help us and our young people to think biblically. We will begin to ask questions like 'What's the biblical view here?' – and that's a very healthy way of thinking.

- Studying Christian doctrine helps our study elsewhere. Christian doctrines are the building blocks, the foundations of the Christian faith, and so studying them gives a good framework for understanding other parts of the Bible. Teaching doctrine will force us out of the prison of Paul's epistles, and we may even find ourselves in the uncharted territories of some of the more obscure parts of the Old Testament.

It's historical

Throughout church history the Christian faith has been taught either by the exposition of Bible passages, or by teaching Christian doctrines from the Bible. Christians throughout history have clearly seen the value in both, as they complement rather than compete with each other.

It's normal

We all believe certain things about God, and the way he works in the world. We have all got some Christian doctrine. Teaching some doctrine is therefore only doing what we all do most of the time, only being open about it – and probably doing it more clearly and in more depth.

It makes a change

We need variety within each week's teaching, and also across the weeks. So to have a couple of sesssions on doctrine in the middle of a term spent mostly on exposition makes a nice change.

Special Two
Important Christian Doctrines

The easiest way to remember these is to recite the Apostles' Creed.

In fact, you could check through the creed to see what doctrines you could cover, and then use the creed to review the progress you have made.

The creed is set out below. Each line could be a single youth group session. But don't plough through the whole lot in one long series. It would make a good 'occasional' series, covering one or two topics a term.

I believe in God, the Father Almighty,
    Creator of heaven and earth.

I believe in Jesus Christ, His only Son, our Lord.
    He was conceived by the power of the Holy Spirit and
        born of the Virgin Mary.

He suffered under Pontius Pilate, was crucified, dead and
        buried.
    He descended to the dead.

On the third day He rose again.
    He ascended into heaven and is seated at the right hand
        of the Father.

He will come again to judge the living and the dead.

I believe in the Holy Spirit.
The Holy Catholic Church,
The communion of saints,
The forgiveness of sins,
The resurrection of the body and life everlasting. Amen.

Or you may want to approach teaching doctrine by compiling a list of major doctrines. They're easy to find: simply look at the contents page of a book of Christian doctrine, such as Bruce Milne's excellent *Know the Truth* (IVP, 1982) Your list might include:

authority	the atonement
revelation	person of the Spirit
Scripture	work of the Spirit
the trinity	identity of the church
human nature	life of the church
humanity of Christ	growth of the church
deity of Christ	

Dangers of doctrine

There are some things to look out for particularly when teaching Christian doctrine:

It's not always straightforward

Some people think that working on doctrine is like doing a jigsaw wearing boxing gloves and a blindfold. It's not quite as difficult as all that, but wouldn't it be easy if Genesis dealt with the doctrine of God, Exodus with man's sin, Leviticus with Old Testament references to Christ, and so on?

Unfortunately the Bible isn't written like that, so we find, for example, references to God's character in almost every book of the Bible. That means some Sherlock Holmes work for us, but it makes a pleasant change from getting firmly strapped into Mark's gospel for weeks on end.

People disagree

– about almost everything, or so it seems. So how can we know what's right when so many people disagree about basic Christian doctrines? Here are three guidelines:

First, follow the principles in chapters 3–4.

Second, take note of what the Bible-believing experts say.

Third, if there is still disagreement, or you are still not sure, don't worry too much.

Christians can differ on some subjects where the truth and integrity of the Gospel is not at stake. Where that's the case, we need love, understanding and patience – and so do they!

It's full of jargon

More than in any other area of Christian teaching, when dealing with doctrine, jargon jumps out in all shapes and forms. 'Justification', 'santification', 'salvation', and other such words are often apparently incomprehensible. Or, more dangerously, we come across words or phrases where we think we know what they mean, but actually we don't. Words like 'grace' and 'peace', and phrases like 'in Christ' and 'through the blood', fall into this category.

Jargon is not necessarily a bad thing. Christian doctrine is useful for accurate and concise communication between Christians. That is always assuming that both parties know what the jargon means.

So translate all the jargon which you come across into language which young people can understand, but at the same time maintain the original truth. And that is potentially tricky. Try translating 'sin', 'salvation' and 'hope' into the language of one of your youth group. Or else use the jargon, but explain and illustrate it, in order to make it clear.

It Looks Boring

To a young person, 'doctrine' probably sounds off-putting. But with very little effort, doctrine can be made far more accessible. A good start would be to change the title on the programme card from 'Christian Doctrines' to 'Body-Building Beliefs', or 'The Facts of the Matter', or 'Believe It or Not'.

Teaching Christian doctrine – some ideas

There isn't only one right method of communicating God's truth to young people. Therefore the following are simply guidelines to help you communicate Christian doctrine to your group:

Do It Yourself

Following the idea that we can't lead people further than we are ourselves, it would be a good idea if we 'did' a little Christian doctrine. Start with a concordance matched to your version of the Bible. Set aside some time each week and be prepared for a little bit of hard work, and a lot of reward.

Get Your Church Doing It

Of course it shouldn't just be the youth leaders who are doing it, and not just the young people who are being taught it. Why not go and see your minister and discuss how the learning of doctrine can be encouraged in your church?

Do Prepare Carefully

There are two areas to bear in mind here:

First, be clear what you want to teach. The great temptation is to try to cover too much in one session. Instead aim to teach one thing, well. So, for example, teach one aspect of sin – that it separates us from God – and teach it properly. Come back to sin in three weeks' time, and teach how it spreads, etc.

Second, poorly prepared sessions on doctrine inevitably end up as paper-chases, with members foraging through the Bible for a series of references. Be well prepared with good activities, games and exercises which all back up and teach the one main point you want to get across.

Try To Apply All You Do

The best way of making doctrine feel dry and irrelevant is never to apply it. This makes a purely academic exercise, satisfying our thirst for knowledge, but leaving everything else in need of refreshment. Some things are hard or even impossible to apply, but always try to show the implications of what you are studying.

Doctrine must make a difference to the way we live, or there is no point in studying it. So, for example, belief in the sudden and unexpected nature of the second coming should be a great incentive to holy living now, being ready for Jesus' return at all times. Apply it and help your young people see how relevant it is today.

Key Example One
Sin – The Heart of the Matter

INTRODUCTION

Before using this with your group, note the following on why we suggest what we suggest . . .

Aim for this session

This is still pithy and memorable and helps to focus what needs to be communicated. This helps in clearer thinking, clearer teaching and clearer understanding.

Notes for leaders

Don't try to be too brave/optimistic and try to cover some of the great Christian doctrines in one session. It's hard to do 'Sin' in one session, and this one could easily be split into two.

Warm-up

Use every possible method of concentrating the members' minds on the subject in hand. A black evening would not only be memorable but would focus their thoughts. It could be repeated for the second week on sin.

Getting going

There's no harm in having an occasional 'heavier than usual' teaching evening, and telling our members this, even the week before.

Teaching 1 – the nature of sin

This contains a number of different ideas. Try using this method of dividing up people by the different aspect of a Bible verse or passage in other meetings. Here is an idea which can be adapted to different situations.

Reference to the original language should probably be omitted and should never be used to display your own knowledge. But for older groups it can be a help in understanding the different Bible words used.

Take a break

Be sensitive to group needs at all times. You may well have those who object to giving false information even in a game, so be sensitive to this in your preparation. Note that these games are all on the subject of sin. You'll need to bring this out in the link into and out of playing these games.

Teaching 2 – the extent of sin

Be clear what you want to teach, and use a memorable method like a disgusting salty cake. Make sure they know why you did it!

Keep variety – hence the verses on the OHP or around the room: group members can help in preparing these.

Teaching 3 – the effects of sin

This could be done by a straight talk or by using the group involvement method. But the latter may need some clear guidance from the leader, so proper preparation is vital.

THE SESSION

Teaching point

To teach that everyone naturally rebels against God and that this damages all relationships.

Briefing

This is the first of two sessions on sin. Although it is possible to do just one of the sessions on its own, you will find it far more helpful to do both of them, as they form an integrated whole and are intended to complement each other.

This session looks at the nature, extent and effects of sin. The second focuses on the Fall in Genesis 3.

The subject matter is fairly heavy. Keep it moving. Don't make the session any heavier than it needs be by being over-long.

Warm-up

As your members arrive, have a graffiti board titled 'What's wrong with the World?' in a prominent place. Have some pens available, and ask for contributions. You may like to start the ball rolling yourself with some witty and humorous comment.

Another possibility is to have a 'Black Evening'. As one of the effects of sin is death, have as many black things as possible in the meeting. Ask group members to wear as much black as possible, and do so yourself. Maybe have black edged invitations to the meeting. Have a black border on the OHP and any handouts you use. Only have black tea and coffee and decorate the room with black pieces of paper.

Kick-off

Tell your members that this evening is even more serious than usual. It's relevant for everyone and there are serious consequences for everyone. Draw attention to the graffiti board and point out that no-one suggested that there wasn't anything wrong with the world. This session reveals what the Bible (and therefore God) says is wrong with the world.

First half

The first teaching segment is about the nature of sin. In essence, sin is when we reject God's authority over us and try to put ourselves in God's place.

The Bible uses a number of different words to describe what sin is. The following list translates different words in the original Bible languages (Hebrew or Greek) and therefore all throw distinctive light on what sin is:

Psalm 51:9, Exodus 32:30 – The commonest word for sin in the Old Testament, meaning missing the mark or erring (*chatatth, or chett*)

Proverbs 28:13 – Active rebellion, trespass of God's will (*pesha*)

Leviticus 4:13 – Going astray (*shagah*)

1 Kings 17:18 – To twist or distort giving the idea of guilt which sin produces (*awon*)

Matthew 1:21 – Missing the mark, failure, fault, concrete wrong-doing (*hamartia*)

1 Corinthians 6:8 – Unrighteousness or injustice (*Adikia*)

Romans 4:15 – Breaking the law (*parabasis*)

1 John 3:4 – Lawlessness (*anomia*)

Titus 2:12 – Godlessness (*asebia*)

James 2:10 – Moral stumble (*ptaio*)

Encouraging your members to use the contents page, ask them to look up these references, and see what they have to tell us about what sin is. You could divide up into smaller groups rather than everyone doing a paperchase. Or you could give a short talk outlining the main points above.

If you are using group work try a new way of dividing them up. Ask your group members all to look up Mark 7:21–23, and then assign one of these sins to each member. Then ask all the adulterers to get together, all the deceitful individuals etc. Ask them before they go on to the Bible study, to think of a quick example of their particular sin and then share it (metaphorically!) with other group members.

For the rare groups that could cope with it, we also mention the relevant Hebrew or Greek word, but in the majority of cases you won't want to worry about that!

If you use group work here make sure everyone has a chance to learn from the other groups, and that you are clear what you want them to be finding out, so that when they feed back, no important points are missed out.

Complete this section by pointing to one other very important verse. Psalm 51:4 points to the fact that sin is something we do first and foremost against God. This is very important for our groups to understand. Make sure they have grasped this point.

Half-time

Hand out copies of old newspapers and ask group members working in teams of two or three to tear out anything to do with sin. Ask groups to show the whole group what little they have left over.

Or you could play Whopper. Each group member thinks up four pieces of information about themselves, or four facts which *they* know about but the rest of the group don't (eg a specialist hobby). Three of these pieces of information must be true and one false. The other group members write down the names of the other participants in the order they will give their information, and everyone has to guess and write down which piece of information was the whopper. Score the results.

A variation on this, is to have four pieces of information, or five, but any number could be wrong or right, (so those who object to giving false information don't have to). The other members have to choose the true and false in the same way as before. You could use negative marking to add a little extra fun (ie plus one for a correct answer, minus one for a wrong answer, nought for no answer). See how many end up with a negative score.

Second half

In this second teaching segment we want to start by showing our groups that sin is universal. It affects every part of everyone.

To illustrate this point before turning to the Bible, bake a cake, but add a good deal of salt or food colouring. At this point in the session cut it up and give each member a piece, instructing them not to eat it until you say. On your permission, they all eat and hopefully are all disgusted. (If you can't bake a cake, then try something simpler, like coffee!) Explain that this is a picture of sin. Every piece of cake was infected, so every part of the human personality is infected with sin. Sin affects every part of us – this is 'total depravity' – not that we are as bad as we can be, but that every part of us is affected.

Back up the teaching from the Bible. The key verses here are Romans 3:10, Romans 3:23, Psalm 14:1–3, Isaiah 64:6, which you can put on a OHP or a wallchart.

Sin affects our:–
  Will – John 8:34 (also Romans 7:14–24)
  Mind – Ephesians 4:17, 18
  Affections/emotions – 2 Timothy 3:4 (also see Romans 1:24–27).
  Speech/behaviour – Galatians 5:19–21 (also Mark 7:21–23)
Sin has also affected the core of our personality: –
  Jeremiah 17:9 (also Romans 7:23).

Now move on to the effects of sin. Begin by asking your young people to jot down their own list of the effects of sin, then brainstorm these onto the OHP/wallchart.

Now tell them that the Bible tells us that the effects of sin are actually far wider than they imagine.

Ask your group either individually or in small groups to complete the 'mix and match' on the Group Extra sheets. The correct pairings are:

Sin destroys relationships

With God – unfit for God's presence (Genesis 3:23, Romans 1:18).

– unable to do God's will (John 8:34, Romans 7:15–21)

– unrighteous before God's law (Galatians 3:10, Ephesians 2:1–3).

– insensitive to God's word (2 Corinthians 4:4).

With others – Sin produces conflict, division, prejudice, exploitation, fear, weakness, misunderstanding (Genesis 3:12, 4:1–16).

With myself – Sin results in inner conflict, and man cannot accept himself (Romans 7:23, Genesis 3:7–8).

With the world – The world is affected directly by sin, and mankind now exploits the world selfishly. (Genesis 3:14–17, Romans 8:21–23).

With time – mankind no longer lives for ever, and now faces anxiety in the face of death (Genesis 2:17, Genesis 3:19, Romans 6:23).

(From Bruce Milne's *Know the Truth*)

Final Whistle

It is possible that your members won't have seen how it all applies to them. So try this:

Stress that this is a private exercise, and ask each member to jot down some of their own sins from the last twenty four hours. Suggest areas they may like to think about – school, at home, with friends, at work. They should consider things they have done, and things they have failed to do, things they have said and things they have thought. Use this to recap anything in the session which needs re-emphasising.

Explain that Jesus died to bear the punishment that our

sins deserve, as our substitute, so that we might be forgiven.

Lead your group in a short time of prayer, asking forgiveness for their sins and thanking Jesus for his death. Ask group members to screw up their 'sins', and throw them in a bin. Or best of all, if your group meet in a home with an open fire, throw them on the fire.

Memory verses

'The heart is deceitful above all things and beyond cure. Who can understand it?' (Jeremiah 17:9).

'There is no difference, for all have sinned and fall short of the glory of God' (Romans 3:23).

Equipment

Bibles
Copies of past newspapers, including some tabloids
Graffiti board and pens
Black edged handouts, clothes, etc. for a 'Black Evening'
Binliners for newspaper rubbish
A cake for some other foodstuff with salt in it
OHP or cards for Bible verses
If no OHP, large sheet of paper for brainstorm

Group Extra
Sin Destroys Relationships

The following are the five main effects of sin. Match up the Bible verses with these headings and add your own further comments as necessary.

Effects of Sin   Bible Verses   My Comments

With God –
Unfit for God's presence,
unable to do God's will,
unrighteous before God's law,
insensitive to God's word

With others –
Sin produces conflict,
division, prejudice,
exploitation, fear, weakness,
misunderstanding

With myself –
Sin results in inner
conflict and man cannot
accept himself

With the world –
The world is affected
directly by sin, and
mankind now exploits the
world selfishly

With time –
Mankind no longer lives
forever, and now faces
anxiety in the face of death

Genesis 3:23   Romans 1:18
Genesis 4:1–16   Genesis 3:19
John 8:34   Ephesians 2:1–3
2 Corinthians 4:4   Genesis 3:14–17
Romans 7:23   Romans 7:15–21
Galatians 3:10   Romans 8:21–23
Genesis 2:17   Genesis 3:12
Romans 6:23   Genesis 3:7–8

Key Example Two
Truth Decay

INTRODUCTION

Note the following applications of some of the principles in chapter 7.

Aim for this session

Again this is short, sharp and to the point. One main thrust has been isolated from this chapter in Genesis.

Getting going

When you have two or more sessions on one subject, or when you are looking at consecutive passages, it's wise to link this week's teaching in with last week's, and so to show how the one leads on to and follows on from the other.

Although this is a doctrinal study, we're focusing on one passage, Genesis 3. The previous session gave more of a biblical overview of the subject, enabling more work on one passage this time.

Teaching 1

Although this concentrates on one passage, it's still important to see this in context, hence the desire to read Genesis 1 and 2 as well.

The use of handouts with Right/Wrong statements is a good thought-provoking method, and makes young people look at the passage. This method can be used in many other situations, and is relatively easy to produce in the leader's preparation time. The feedback though is important, for which the leaders need to know their stuff, and be confident in the handout itself. Advance preparation is important, especially if using a published one as in this case.

For the less experienced leader, a short talk is often easier, and good practice. There is nothing wrong with talks as part of a youth group evening.

Take a break

Games like 'Call my Bluff' may be fun, but can go on for too long and inhibit the teaching. So whenever playing a game like this, don't have more than one in an evening, realistically work out the timing beforehand, and watch the clock.

Driving it home

Doctrine is relevant. Sin describes so much of what happens in the world today that not only is it easy to point to the importance and relevance of the subject, it is also very important.

The jigsaw activity helps here, and should serve to show the wide impregnation of sin in today's society.

THE SESSION

Teaching point

Sin is a desire to become like God.

Briefing

This is the second of two sessions on sin.

Beware when covering this subject that it can touch sensitive areas and there may be individuals to follow up personally at the end of the meeting or soon afterwards.

Although this is a doctrinal study, we will be focusing on one particular passage, Genesis 3, as this is central to our understanding of sin.

Warm-up

As the essence of this session is to teach how sin reverses the God-ordained order in the world, you may like to have a 'Back to Front' evening (see p. 119).

Or try playing 'Killer' or 'Cheat'. In 'Killer' the group sit in a circle (ideally in a slightly darkened room), and one is nominated as the killer by being dealt a joker when everyone is dealt a playing card. The killer kills others by winking at them, whereupon the more theatrical come into their own! If the killer is seen in the act, he may be challenged and the game starts again.

'Cheat' is the well-known card game with a variety of different rules, the aim of which is to get rid of your cards.

Or try 'Balloon Stomp'. Give each member a balloon and a length of string. Ask them to blow up the balloon and tie it to one of their ankles with the string. On the word go, they must stomp on everyone else's balloon while protecting theirs. When theirs is stomped, they drop out. At the end, ask what this tells us about the winner!

All these games draw attention to our sin, so move on from here to introduce this session.

Kick-off

Begin by reviewing last week. Ask people what they remembered, and re-make the important points which they've forgotten.

Remind your group that this week is on sin too, continuing on from last week. Introduce them to Genesis 3. The controversy of whether Adam and Eve actually existed as two individuals or whether this is a picture of the state of mankind now, is something of a red herring which you could easily get diverted with. Be prepared to answer it if it comes up, but make sure that you spend the majority of time in this session teaching what Genesis 3 has to say about the state of mankind.

First half

This first teaching segment concentrates on verses 1–13 and the *events* of the Fall. The Second Half covers the rest of the chapter and the *implications* of the Fall.

Begin by reading Genesis 3:1–13.

To put it in context, it would be ideal to read Genesis chapters 1 and 2 as well. This is a large chunk, but if your group are up to it it's well worth the effort. Maybe ask someone with a good reading voice to make a tape of Genesis 1 and 2 and play this at the meeting, for a change.

Give your group copies of the Group Extra sheet. Ask them to complete these either individually or in pairs. Then have an all-together session when you go through the sheets and discuss the answers. You may think this is a little difficult for your group, but some of the questions are easier than others. Give it a try and be prepared to help with the difficulties. This forms the basis of your teaching, so make sure you are properly prepared and know what the correct answers are! The following comments should help.

– The serpent questions the truth of God's word. He misquotes God (v1), he suggests that God is selfish, making petty rules which he demands we keep.

– If we compare verse 3 with Genesis 2:16,17, there is no mention here of 'touching'. Also note that in chapter 2 the command is given to Adam before Eve is formed, and she is quoting what Adam has presumably told her here.

– The serpent's promise to Eve is that she will be like God (v5), which is more than just knowing right from wrong, which she knows anyway.

– Temptation does not equal sin. The serpent does not command.

– There is no mention of an apple.

– Verse 7 reveals Adam and Eve's naivety.

– In Genesis 1 and 2 the order of authority in creation is God – mankind – animals.

– In seeking to become like God, the Fall reverses this order.

– Verses 9–11 don't reveal an ignorant God. Rather, he is trying to get Adam and Eve to admit their sin.

– The essence of sin is trying to take God's place.

– Both Adam and Eve try to blame each other.

If you like, you could use these points as a basis for a short talk, and whether you give a talk or involve the group more, make sure that they grasp that sin is in essence a desire to become like God.

Half time

Play Call my Bluff from the TV panel game. Do some research beforehand and find out some really obscure words (the best place to find these is in the Oxford English Dictionary), and write these out on card together with true and false definitions. If you're really organised, let the participants have the cards beforehand so they have the opportunity of preparing something in advance. Play the game as it happens on TV: two teams, three in a team, and each team takes it in turns to define a word, two of the definitions being bluff, and one true. The other team then have to decide which is true and which is bluff.

What happens in Call my Bluff is that two-thirds of the people lie. Highlight this as you draw out the point of this game.

Second half

In this teaching segment we will look at Genesis 3:14–24. Ask one of your group members to read this out. Number your group off, 1,2,3,1,2,3, etc. In the light of what follows try to make sure as far as possible that 2s are male and 3s are female. Ask all the 1s to investigate the curse on the serpent (vv14-15), the 2s to investigate the curse on the woman (v16), and the 3s that on the man, (vv17–19). Say that you will come as a radio reporter. In a short interview, ask group members for their report on what has happened. Use a tape recorder and microphone – most ghetto blasters have a built in microphone, so ask one of your group members to bring theirs and help you out if necessary. It would be even better to use a camcorder and play it back on the TV. Maybe someone in your church has got one that you could borrow.

Give your group four minutes to work out what difference the Fall has made to them as a serpent, man or woman from the passage. Then with the tape recorder or video record a brief introduction from you, giving the outline of verses 1–13 (First Half) stressing that sin is in essence a desire to become like God. Then interview a small selection of serpents, men and women. Play back the results.

Complete the teaching by describing this new government, the government of man. This is a government of:

- **Deceit.** It started and continues with lies.
- **Darkness.** We have placed ourselves under the rule of Satan. This is not just a one-off act but a continuing rebellion involving everyone today (see Romans 5:12).
- **Death.** Man is banished from God's presence. God is the source of life and so man is rejecting life. (See Genesis 3:21–24).
- **Decay.** The whole physical world is involved in decay because of the fall. But this decay is not total. God still cares for fallen man (Genesis 3:21) and his hand is still at work in creation (eg rain, growth of crops, etc).

Final Whistle

Cut up an OHP acetate or large piece of card into jigsaw-shaped pieces, one for each member. Give each group member one piece of card or acetate and an appropriate pen (divide into small groups if your group is too large for this).

Make sure they know which side of the acetates/card they are required to write on (write a number or word on this yourself before you give them out), and then ask group members to write on their acetate evidence from today's world that Genesis 3 is right. They should give specific examples of sin in the world today. Construct the jigsaw and make suitable comments. Ask group members privately and individually to note down areas where they are easily tempted to believe (and then to act upon), the lie that God doesn't know best, and/or the lie that God has been unfair to me. And most important, ask group members to note down where they have tried to take the place of God, shutting him out, and trying to rule their own life.

As last week, explain the death of Jesus, dying in our place for our sin, and pray together as you close, asking for God's forgiveness and thanking him for his Son.

Memory Verse

'For God knows that when you eat of it your eyes will be opened, and you will be like God, knowing good and evil.' Genesis 3:5.

Leadership ideas

Try not to do all the teaching yourself. In situations such as Second Half, it's far better to have one leader concentrating on reporting while one concentrates on the points which need to be taken up, and makes notes for the next part of the session.

Equipment

Copies of Group Extra sheets
Bibles or copies of Genesis 3
Playing cards for Killer

Cassette recorder and microphone, or camcorder/TV
OHP and pens
Cardboard/acetate cut into jigsaw shaped pieces
Balloons and string

Group Extra
Genesis 3:1–13
Right or Wrong?

Tick or cross each statement.

1 The serpent's strategy is to cast doubt on the truth of God's words and motives.

2 In verse 3 Eve exaggerates God's command.

3 The serpent promises Eve that if she eats the fruit she'll be able to tell right from wrong.

4 The serpent commands Eve to eat the forbidden fruit.

5 Eve ate the apple first, then Adam.

6 Adam and Eve's naivety was destroyed by eating from the tree.

7 Sin reverses the order of creation: God – Mankind – Animals to become Animals – Mankind – God.

8 In verse 9 God doesn't know where Adam and Eve are, and in verse 11 God doesn't know whether Adam and Eve have eaten the forbidden fruit.

9 The essence of Adam and Eve's sin is to try and take God's place, becoming like him.

10 Both Adam and Eve deny responsibility for their sin.

8

Flavour of the Month
– Looking at Contemporary Issues

Last Friday evening All Hallows youth group were looking at Aids. That was the first of a mini-series on human sexuality. Tonight it's 'Homosexuality', followed the week after that by 'Masturbation'. They are pretty keen on looking at issues facing young people today at All Hallows. And their with-it, keen and enthusiastic youth leaders are all well researched and know their topics well. The members at All Hallows are now a fount of all wisdom on these subjects.

But one slightly anxious parent commented; 'By the end of this series, my fourteen-year-old will know more about sex than I ever will.' Some of the older members wonder whether it's a social worker training course, but admit to being fascinated by it anyway. Another parent, who happens to be the churchwarden at All Hallows, is more concerned that, 'There's nothing much Christian about what they have been learning in the last few weeks. And anyway, they learn all that stuff at school, don't they?'

In the middle of last week, the youth leaders from All Hallows went to a training evening organised by the local Baptist church. They had a great time, and met two of the leaders from the new Methodist youth group in town, who wanted to know what All Hallows had on their current programme. When the Methodists heard, they were pretty surprised, because they had both been reading a book stressing that youth leaders were Bible teachers. They hadn't even thought that you could tackle issues like this. The new Methodist youth leaders went home that evening with their eyes opened, but slightly concerned that the youth group at All Hallows could look at all these issues but not even mention the Bible.

Looking at today's issues is a very popular way of working with young people. But it's not necessarily a Christian way of working. Plenty of secular youth clubs have discussion groups with the same approach, and they do a very valuable job.

But Christian youth work should be distinct from secular youth work. Sadly, though, newcomers would often be hard-pressed to tell the difference, as we begin the serious bit of the evening with: 'Right, what shall we discuss tonight then?'

So what's the difference? How should a Christian youth group look at current issues affecting them and the world around them?

1 The task in hand

In most of the book so far, the starting point has been the Bible, and after having understood it properly, it is then applied to the world in which we and our young people live.

In this chapter, this way of working is reversed. Here, the starting point is the world, and then we see what the Bible has to say about it.

In looking at the world, we want to bring the Bible to bear.

Important Questions

That immediately raises a number of questions. Has the Bible got anything to say? Is it relevant? How can the Bible possibly have anything to say on issues which weren't even dreamt of when the Bible was written?

In thinking about these questions, bear in mind these assertions:–

The Bible is God's word for all time

It is God preaching, speaking, communicating. It is by nature, eternal, so expect to hear God speaking when it is read today, and when you teach it to your group. Because of it's nature, the Bible is relevant today.

> The Bible has always been authoritative for Christians – both for developing the Christian mind and guiding Christian behaviour (David Atkinson, *Pastoral Ethics in Practice*).

The Bible is sufficient

It tells us all we need in order to live lives which are pleasing to God at the end of the 20th Century.

The task for all Christians is to read it and put it into practice.

> Your word is a lamp to my feet and a light for my path (Psalm 119:105).

The Bible is contemporary

It's very easy to write off the Bible as an ancient relic. In fact it covers many of today's big issues directly. If, for instance, you are covering marriage and divorce, homosexuality, materialism, the occult or many other issues, the Bible has a lot of specific things to say.

The Bible may appear to be silent

There are issues where the Bible has nothing directly to say. And any reasonable person wouldn't expect it to. AIDS and the Media aren't in the Bible, and you wouldn't expect them to be. But promiscuity, manipulation, greed, and our sexual behaviour are there, and are highly relevant when we are looking at Aids and the Media. The Bible gives principles for Christian living, and it's right to seek to apply these wisely to issues where the Bible is otherwise silent.

The Bible has one mind and voice

It is the work of one divine author, working through many different human writers, and it is consistent and has one view on current issues. Contradictions, discrepancies and difficulties are apparent, but there is usually a fairly straightforward answer to these. Where the Bible doesn't give clear guidelines on a contemporary issue, then the best way forward with our groups is to say what different Christians believe on this matter, to give our own opinion, and to stress that Christians differ legitimately on this.

Thinking Biblically

The task is to help young people to think biblically, or
Christianly, in order to develop a Christian mind. This means
thinking the same way as the Bible does. It's a wider and more
important task than just teaching a Christian response to, say,
environmental issues. They will also begin to see everything
through Christian spectacles, and begin to think at all times from a
Christian perspective. That's a gradual long term development.
But it's far more significant and far more helpful to your young
people than just telling them, for example, that a Christian
shouldn't go out with a non-Christian. Over time, as they begin to
think biblically, they will begin to see that for themselves, and to
understand why. Of course in the meantime, we need to be
teaching about Christians' relationships with non-Christians. But
we also need to be teaching our young people how to think
through these things for themselves. Have a look at Special One,
'Thinking Straight', for more ideas on thinking biblically and what
it means.

Gifts to Help our Thinking

It is possible to teach young people how to think biblically. In
doing that, and in all work with young people we need to
remember that God has given us four gifts.

- **A mind.** We are all rational and intelligent creatures. The fact
  that some have better minds than others doesn't mean that those
  with poorer minds are absolved from using them. Your heart
  may beat better than mine, but thankfully mine still bothers to
  beat.

  > Therefore, I urge you, brothers, in view of God's mercy, to
  > offer your bodies as living sacrifices, holy and pleasing to God –
  > this is your spiritual act of worship. Do not conform any longer
  > to the pattern of this world, but be transformed by the renewing
  > of your mind. Then you will be able to test and approve what
  > God's will is – his good, pleasing and perfect will (Romans
  > 12:1).

• **The Bible.** To direct our thinking. The Bible is God's great revelation.

• **The Holy Spirit.** Who opens the Bible and gives us understanding, both of what it means, and how it should apply. The word and the Spirit are inseparably linked in the Bible. We need both.

• **The Church.** The context of our thinking and teaching is God's people. They set a marvellous safeguard against foolish or wrong thinking.

Special One
Thinking Straight

'If we want to live straight, we have to think straight'. John Stott, *Issues Facing Christians Today*

What is distinctive about thinking as a Christian?

There are certain things which we believe about God and man which affect what we think as Christians about issues such as Aids, sex, politics and the like. These key points are central to the Christian faith, and not only do we believe them, but they should also affect the way we think. Each key point is important, although for any particular issue, some points will be more relevant than others.

When thinking about a new issue, try asking how the following affect the way a Christian should react to it. Two main books have greatly helped my thinking here H Blamires, *The Christian Mind* (SPCK) and J R W Stott, *Issues Facing Christians Today*, (Marshall). Christians believe in:

1 The supernatural
This world is not all that there is. There is a whole spiritual world of good and evil, and we either follow and serve the good or the evil. Both God and the Devil are real.

2 God the Creator

God is the creator of the world. He has ultimate power, and as our creator, has ultimate authority over us. He has given mankind responsibility for creation.

3 The Fall

Man has rebelled against God's authority, and sin is a major and significant factor in the way the world operates today.

4 Redemption

In Jesus' death and resurrection, God has done all that is necessary to save mankind from his wrath. The cross is the model for how Christians should live in the world. It should overshadow and influence all that we are and do.

5 Concern for people

The two basic and summary commandments for the Christians are to love God, and to love others.

People are important to the Christian, and we must remember God's love for individuals, which we should mirror.

6 Truth and authority

There are such things as ultimate truth and authority, and therefore absolute right and wrong, which are determined by God. Our examination of issues must seek to find the truth by thinking biblically about the subject.

7 Second Coming and judgement

The Christian life has a future orientation. Christianity is about preparing us for heaven, and saving us from condemnation at the judgement. This revelation and universal acknowledgement of God's rule must influence our thinking about issues today.

---

2 Teaching Issues – How?

The following questions apply both to overall programme planning and the actual preparation of a particular session. They are designed to help think through how a particular issue can be taught, and to enable this to be done in the most relevant and helpful way.

a) *How much?*

. . . of a particular issue can I cover in one teaching session?

Most issues are pretty large-scale, and to cover them thoroughly would take far more than one week's teaching session. For instance, if you look at 'Sex and the Christian' in one session, you will almost inevitably end up with broad and probably vague statements. So narrow down the scope of each session. Even if the title is broad, be clear what it is you wish to focus on. Subjects have to be defined narrowly to have maximum impact.

b) *Why?*

. . . is this an issue for my young people? Or if it isn't, why should it be?

Maybe it's not. I can remember as a teenager sitting in relationships talks which almost always started with, 'Marriage – the ideal'. I was just waiting for the bit on 'how far can we go?'. Marriage just wasn't an issue for me at the time.

On the other hand, it could have been presented as 'something to think about now because it's important for your future', and 'you can't understand sex unless you see where it lives'. Marriage needs to be an issue for young people today, because they can't think biblically about sex until they understand about marriage.

More positively, it's also good to think over why certain things are so important for young people. So, for instance, why are friends so important to them? Why is their appearance so vital? Why are they so interested in the relationship talk? As we put ourselves in their trainers, we'll be better at understanding what their concerns are.

c) *When?*

. . . did I last cover this issue, and when will I next do it? And when I last did it, what did I say?

Some issues suffer from over-exposure. Or more accurately, some youth groups suffer from over-exposure to the same issues.

So don't overdo it.

The job of the youth leader is not to produce budding members of Greenpeace, but to be teaching young people God's word and helping them to think biblically about everyday life. Clearly some issues are more important to young people than others, and we should be helping them think biblically about areas that are important to them. Equally the less important areas shouldn't be neglected.

It's a case of look before you leap.

d) *Who?*

. . . will be there, and who can help in my preparation?

Bear in mind the group members as you plan and prepare, taking their specific needs into consideration.

But also look for help. Who can help you prepare? Why not ask one of the group members? After all, they have an intimate knowledge of the way young people think, and what the important issues are for them.

It's also a great help to talk to others, like your minister, and other group leaders. Talking sharpens ideas and clarifies issues.

But that, of course, assumes you are preparing far enough ahead to allow time for it!

e) *Which?*

. . . published resources will be of most help to me?

There is a whole range of good Christian books looking at issues from the perspective of Christian young people. They are worth the investment, either personally or as a youth group or church. If your group has its own account, one good way of spending some of this money is by building up a small library of resource books for current and future leaders. These books can also be lent to members.

Recommendations include:

John Stott, *Issues Facing Christians Today* (Marshall Pickering 1984, 1991).

David Atkinson, *Pastoral Ethics in Practice* (Monarch, 1989).

The excellent *Frameworks* series published by IVP, aimed at young people themselves (sixteen years and older), and covering a very wide range of subjects, including 'careers', 'sex', 'films' and the media.

The *Young People and . . .* series published by Kingsway, by various authors, so far covering young people and drugs, sex, the bomb, aids, and the occult. This has now been republished as *You and . . .*

The *You Decide* series published by Scripture Union, covering 'love and sex', 'war and pacifism', and 'racism'.

f) Which?

. . . Bible principles are relevant?
. . . Bible passages do I want to use?
First, decide which Bible principles are central, peripheral or just don't feature at all. God's people and published resources will be a great help here, and as this is the real nitty gritty of the preparation, it will need time.

Remember two things at this stage:

- **Do distil.** Don't make it too complicated, and aim to make one point well.

- **Don't distract.** Remember that you want to help your group members think biblically. That means that six proof texts on global warming will be of less use than six biblical principles on man's duty to be responsible for creation, which could be applied not only to global warming but many other specific areas too.

  Aim to summarise those six biblical principles under one overall headline for the evening's meeting.

Second, decide on particular Bible passages which illustrate the biblical principles that you want to get across.
Make sure:

- There aren't too many verses/passages. Six at the most, preferable fewer.

- None of the chosen verses repeat themselves.

- You are clear and specific as to what they are saying. Look at the contexts carefully, and don't be vague. What *precisely* is this saying?

- You put to one side verses which don't back up the principle you are wanting to make.

Avoid seeking out proof texts to justify an argument, while failing to recognise why the Bible was written, the circumstances of writing, who wrote it, etc.

And do avoid the opposite approach, which says that some or all of the Bible is irrelevant for today because of the cultural gap between then and now. Have a look at chapters three and four for more details on this.

> Aim to teach a few biblical principles which can be summarised by one catch headline. Illustrate each principle with a carefully chosen verse or passage from the Bible.
> Then apply what you've learned to the issue.

g) *What?*

. . . is the main teaching point?

As always, it's vital to isolate one memorable and accurate point for members to remember at the end of the teaching evening. Call it a 'Headline' or a 'Teaching Point' – it's what you want them to go away with.

They will probably only easily remember one main thing from the evening, so make sure it's *you* who decides what it is that they remember.

h) How?

ed

...am I going to get this across to my sixteen year old lads who are far more interested in football and girls than in what the Bible has to say on these matters?

Read on ...

Special Two
Pitfalls

---

1 Boredom

It's very easy for issue-led meetings to go on too long. There's so much material to cover, that you try to do too much and overrun.

Be realistic and prune. Avoid general titles which will tempt you into trying to cover too much.

2 Issue-ism

This is where you look at the issue but not the Bible.

After all, sex is an interesting subject, and so is materialism. So it's very easy to spend most, if not all of the session looking at these fascinating subjects, and not actually looking at the Bible. The youth leader's job is to help their young people think biblically about the issue, and that means biblical input from you. Don't let the issue blind you. Instead look at it through the eyes of the Bible.

3 Bias

We all have our hobby horses. We all *think* we know the biblical line on hot issues. And we're very good at being biased. That's because we have preconceived ideas, or we haven't prepared properly, or we haven't had time to think it through, or because we've simply left out some key Bible verses. You can minimise the chance of bias by being open to learn new things, and by working hard at the preparation.

4 The Prince Charming syndrome – where you and your group can get carried away

Young people can feel strongly about things, and on some subjects, once they start it's hard to stop them. That may not be a bad thing, but equally, heated arguments are superb at closing the mind to what the Bible is *really* saying.

So think ahead, spot the controversial or heated subjects, and decide on ways to cover them which will reduce the heated discussion or prevent it happening in the first place.

5 Confusion

It's fine saying that we need to think biblically, but how about those contradictions? How, for example can we talk about a Christian attitude to war, when the God of the Old Testament seems to be a warmonger, but the God of the New Testatment seems to be a peacemonger?

How about those subjects where the Bible is silent?

Again this boils down to thorough preparation. The confuson in our minds is cleared up as we work hard, talk to others, pray, think and spend time reading. Then when we are clear in our own minds, we can begin to see how this can be communicated to others.

---

3 Teaching Issues – Methods

There is no foolproof system for teaching a Christian approach to current day issues, or for teaching young people to think biblically about them. But the following guidelines may be of some use:

a) Be relevant

Start with the issue and point out how relevant it is. This should be relatively easy because you will usually be dealing with issues which produce some spark amongst young people. They will naturally be interested. The difficulties come when the leader is intent on investigating his pet theory which no one else finds interesting.

b) Be honest

Explain what the issues are for a Christian. Show what difficulties the world's view of this issue presents to someone who is a Christian. Give a main headline or teaching point for the session.

It is often good to introduce a personal note or give other examples here. Perhaps a case study, real life account or illustration would bring the issue home to people and get them thinking about how this particular issue might affect them.

c) Be thought-provoking

It's easy not to be. Add spice by relating everything you say to individuals. Earth it. Give concrete examples. Do your homework and come up with facts and figures, but translate these into every-day teenage language so that they can relate to what you are saying.

Drive the point home, and try and get the group members to put themselves in the shoes of, say, a drug addict, a homeless person, a single parent, etc.

d) Be biblical

A meeting which is relevant, honest and thoughtful needn't necessarily be Christian. So be biblical too.

We want the group to begin to think biblically about the subject, or at the very least to see what the Bible and therefore God, have to say about it.

Biblical input can be given straight, from the front. Or you can use group work or hands-on Bible study. This is where the members do their own research, helped and directed by the leaders, and using commentaries, concordances and other Bible study aids.

Whichever methods you use (see chapter 2 for a lot more), at the end of the day ask of the meeting, 'Was it biblical?'

e) Be practical

The Bible is always relevant, and particularly so here, because we're starting with the world and seeing how the Bible applies to it. So half the job of application is done already. But don't leave the job half done.

What should the group *do* as a result of the meeting? What difference should the meeting make to their lives? God doesn't speak purely to pamper our desire for knowledge. He speaks so that we will listen and change our lives as a result. So each week have an aim which specifically relates to what you want the members to *do* as a result of the meeting.

Key Example One

The Media – Watch Them with your Eyes Open

INTRODUCTION

Please read the following before you use this key example with your group.

Teaching point

This is a specific point, highlighting the possible negative influence of the media. Make sure the teaching point is as specific as possible.

Briefing

Note again that this is not a secular meeting to inform, but a Christian meeting to teach the young people how to think biblically about the subject.

Warm-up

This introduces the evening by looking at the media in a general way. It gets the young people thinking about the subject.

First half

Structure is important as it helps to give clear understanding and therefore make the point clearly.

This part also aims to bring home to the young people the influence of the media by opening their eyes to their prevalence and influence in society. The use of the 'Media Consumption Chart' and the advertising slogans aim to do this. If you are using the advertising slogans, use your own, up-to-date ones.

Don't spend too long on the 'First Half', and run out of time for the more important 'Second half'.

'Half-time'

As this is a session on the media, it would be worth the extra effort to use as many of the modern methods as you can. So for instance, if it's at all possible to get hold of a video and television, then this would be a good session to use these.

Second half

Don't leave this out, as it's the most important part of the session. And do prepare the Bible passages carefully. Choose which ones you will use, and make sure you understand them in context.

Final whistle

While making practical suggestions, don't put words into their mouths. Leave the decision making up to the group members themselves. We hope and pray that they will change as a result of the meetings, but let them make the precise application.

Extra time

Don't use these as well as the other ideas. There is far too much material in this session already. So if you want to use one of these ideas, leave out something else.

THE SESSION

Teaching point

The considerable and possibly negative influence of the media for the Christian.

Group action

spints

Aim that the group should begin to develop the ability to <u>critically</u> assess the media they 'consume' and adjust their consumption of them accordingly.

Briefing

Young people can get a lot of negative input from Christians about the media. In this session try and be positive as well as negative. Media influence on us is not all bad. There are good elements too, although we do need to keep our eyes open to the unhelpful and negative influences.

All the way through, keep clearly in mind the need to be viewing this from a Christian perspective. This isn't a secular meeting to inform about the media, but a Christian one to help our young people think Christianly about them.

Warm-up

Ask your group to think up some obscure fact about themselves which no-one else in the group knows, and then turn this into a newspaper headline: perhaps a tabloid headline, but preferably not from 'The Sun'!

why not?

Ask them to write this down on a slip of paper and then one of the leaders writes these headlines onto the OHP/large sheet of card. Ask the rest of the group to decide which headline refers to which person.

Kick-off

By outlining what the media are, and which aspects you will be focusing on in this week's session. This material looks at the influence of TV/radio, newspapers, magazines and adverts in general. You may want to draw examples from just one of these, or take material from other areas such as films, books, etc.

First half

a) The influence of the media

Stress that the media are a very strong influence on most of us because of the amount we consume, and the power of them. Ask your group individually to fill in a copy of the media consumption chart (see Group Extra sheet). Then compare notes and prepare to be amazed at the amount that we consume. Compare your group's results with the average UK/weekly media consumption of seventy-five hours per person. Other statistics include the fact that the British spend eighty hours per week watching soap, and that five to fourteen year olds spend an average of twenty three hours per week watching the television, so that by their late teens they have witnessed 16,000 violent deaths on the screen.

The proliferation of satellite dishes and cable TV means a far wider choice of viewing, and the increasing number of televisions and videos means that programmes can be recorded and watched several times at the viewer's convenience. You may like to ask how many of your group have one, two or three televisions in their house, and one, two or three VCRs.

Second, stress the power of the media, and especially that the media are not only part of our society, but actually change society. The media affect what we buy, how we spend our time, what is important to us, what we eat and drink, etc. Newspapers not only reflect public opinion, they shape it.

There are plenty of examples to draw from our own experience here. One particularly good one is the way that the Smirnoff Vodka advertising campaign, targeted at younger people, has actually changed people's drinking habits so much that vodka is now a common drink for many in their twenties and thirties.

The media also becomes part of our everyday language. Show your group this by giving them the following advertising slogans verbally, or on a hand-out, or visually on a card/OHP. Then ask them to match the company or product with the slogan. They'll probably find it very easy.

1   'Vorsprung durch Technik'
2   'The ultimate driving machine'
3   'The world's favourite airline'
4   'Reaches the parts . . .'
5   'We're getting there'
6   'We are. Are you?'
7   'Why sail across when you can cruise across?'
8   'The mild cigar, from . . .'
9   'It's you we answer to.'
10   'Buy into what you plug into.'

Some of these may now be out of date, so replace them with more contemporary ones.

b) The negative influence the media can have

Show your group some adverts. Cut them out of magazines or newspapers, or if you can, video a selection from the television. Ask your group:

- *What kind of message do they portray?* An ideal world? Greed? Materialism? I'll be OK if I have this product? I'll be accepted if I have this product?
- *Are there sexual stereotypes?* Many adverts use sex to sell their products. That's not what God intended sex for!
- *What unspoken communication is going on?* The media SAY much more than is spoken, and much of this is very powerful.
- *Are these giving an honest and real view of what the world is really like?* Many adverts give a distorted and idealised view of the world, and so distort people's perception of reality.

This distortion of reality is common to all the media. Partly it's due to the fact that unbiased reporting is impossible. The reporter/ advert maker/programme maker is BOUND to influence us by their own thoughts and ideas, their choice of words, by the camera angle, etc. But some distortion is intended. To show this, buy several different, contrasting newspapers, and cut out their reports of the same event. Pin these reports together, and give each selection of reports to your group to see how different the newspaper reports can be. Ask your group why this is the case. And then discuss the power which the media can have on us, and whether these reports are actually telling the truth.

Half-time

Give your group a selection of magazine adverts, or watch some television, or listen to the radio (either live, or – safer – pre-recorded and selected by you).

Ask your group which of the following values were reflected in the excerpts.

Tick each one as many times as ~~it is mentioned.~~ *you notice it*

1 Wealth, luxury, greed.
2 Security.
3 Sex or physical attractiveness.
4 Intelligence.
5 Conformity.
6 Justice.
7 Power, strength.
8 Responsibility.
9 Ego/pride.
10 Escapism.
11 Ease, comfort.
12 Freedom from responsibility.
13 Status.
14 Other.

Discuss this as a group, and try to draw conclusions about what the media say to us, and whether their values are helpful or unhelpful for the Christian.

Second half

Begin the second half by asking your group to fill in Group Extra chart 2, 'How you see it'.

But the media can also be a good influence.

- The media can highlight wrongs in society and help us remove them. [eg child abuse, third world starvation]

• The media can be good entertainment helping us use leisure time wisely by relaxing.

But what is the Christian response? Try the following outline for a brief talk:

a) Be aware

Don't assume all the media are 'fit for Christian consumption'. Make sure your group keep their eyes open and think about it. It may be anti-Christian material which they are consuming. It can spread stereotypes which are unhelpful to Christians, and the subtle unchristian or anti-Christian messages can be very persuasive.

b) Be biblical

Focus on Philippians 4, and first look at verses 12 and 19. From these, teach about Paul's learning to be content. Advertising agencies would never have this as their motto!

Second, look at verse 8, and teach the importance of fixing your minds on the good things, rather than on the dubious. What Christians think about is very important, and the media influence our thinking a good deal. What goes into our minds controls our thinking, so be positive too, and teach the importance of Christian input into our minds. Use Romans 12:1,2 to teach the importance of renewing our minds.

Third, the media throw into question where our treasure should be stored up. The media pander to human greed, so a careful study of Matthew 6:20–21 would be valuable, focusing on the impermanence and frailty of earthly goods compared with heavenly goods, and the dangerous effect which earthly goods have on our hearts.

Fourth, careful study of Colossians 3:1–11 will be valuable. You may choose to establish first some principles of Christian living: that it starts with the fact of what Christ has achieved for us (v3), so we have our hearts and minds set in the right place (vv1–2); and all the Christian life is lived in the shadow of the future coming of Christ (v4).

With this in mind, then, we can begin to be practical, putting to death and ridding ourselves of all that belongs to our sinful nature (vv5 ff). Then ask your group (perhaps in threes?) to consider what this has to say about our media consumption, and ask them to be as specific and detailed as possible.

c) Be cautious

Point out that the media consume a great deal of precious time.

Note too that the influence of the media can be slow, subtle and insidious, changing Christian minds so that they think the same way the world does. Get your group thinking, 'What is the media doing to me?'

Stress now that we need to 'watch the media with our eyes open'.

Final Whistle

Ask your group to consider how their attitude to the media should change. Make practical suggestions such as cutting down on the amount of TV, and using the time more usefully, or suggest a campaign of letter writing to the local or national papers or TV/radio if an issue has arisen in a meeting. Media chiefs do apparently take complaints seriously.

You may like to instigate a media review in your youth group every so often where you look at the values and impact of addictive programmes, and assess them from a Christian perspective.

Ask your group members to make a private written note of one thing which this evening's session will change, and one area where their eyes have been opened and which they will view differently from now on.

Leadership ideas

It's very easy in this session to look at the media, but not to look at them Christianly. So as you select and adapt from this material, make sure all the Bible material is included, and in the group session stress that you want to look at the media from a specifically Christian perspective.

Extra Time

1 **Election time.** First draw up a list of favourite TV programmes, newspapers, magazines, films in the last year, adverts on TV, radio DJs, videos, etc. Make sure that your list includes all those that are appropriate to your group, and then ask members to vote for their favourite, or better still, their top three in each category. Why not give them six votes to be placed, three for the top, two for the second, one for the third. Use the election to draw up a list of group favourites.

2 In First Half, instead of using the advertising slogans, ask a group member to record advertising jingles from TV adverts, but to leave out the product, and ask your group to guess the products. They will probably find it easy.

3 In First Half again, while looking at the negative power of the media, you may want to use a VCR to record the opening moments of several soap operas (starting with the signature tune, but stopping just before the first words are spoken). Ask your group what these excerpts have *said* so far by the images they have portrayed, before a word is spoken.

Equipment

Group Extra sheets
OHP/sheet of card and pens
Copies of a variety of newspaper reports of the same incident
Video snippets of adverts

Group Extra
My Media Consumption

Type of medium	Hours p/w average
TV	
Radio	
Newspapers	
Magazines	
Adverts (eg hoardings, trains)	
Films	
Books	
Other	

How You See It

Topic	How the media see it	How the Bible sees it
Sex		
The family		
Success		
Relationships		
Marriage		
God		
Christianity		

Key Example Two
Materialism – A Twentieth Century God

INTRODUCTION

Teaching point/Group action

Be as specific as possible. Keep them in mind as you prepare and lead this session. Always try to take the group back to these several times during the session.

Warm-up

This raises the issue of materialism in young people's minds, and helps you introduce the session. If you can afford to, use the £5 note, as this shows young people how attractive money is. Don't leave this part out completely it helps focus on the issue.

Kick-off

Tell your young people the outline of the evening, as the structure helps memory. It also gives the members an idea of the shape of the session, and encourages you to keep to it!

First half/Second half

This is the core of the session. Don't try to cover too much, superficially. It's far better to do less, in depth. So select one or two passages from First Half. But still use one of the different methods suggested.

If members investigate the passage themselves, be sure to give a short, clear summary, as suggested at the end of First Half. This will clarify the issues for your members.

In Second Half prepare the Luke 16 passage carefully. Think it through. Do you agree with this interpretation? Why? You don't have to agree with every book you read!

Half-time

This gives group members a lighthearted way of focusing on the subject. Beware of the time factor though.

Final whistle

This aims to help members apply the Bible principles. It will only really work if you have covered Luke 16.

THE SESSION

Teaching point

God gives us possessions to use for his benefit, not just for ours.

Group Action

Aim that the group will develop a godly attitude to things and begin to use them for God, and especially for the Gospel.

Briefing

This session does not aim to teach just about the Christian use of money. Our use of money is part of the whole area of materialism, and so will be mentioned, but probably should be dealt with specifically in a separate teaching session. This session aims to be more general in looking at the issues raised by materialism in the 20th Century.

Materialism consists in storing up and using things (including money) purely for our own enjoyment and benefit. This never satisfies, and so will always be a frustrating idol, and is the reverse of what the Bible teaches about the use of things. Biblically, all we have should be used for God and none of it should be seen as 'mine'.

Warm-up

As an initial mixer, give someone in your group an amount of money (perhaps a £1 coin, or £5 note), but tell them to keep quiet about this. Then ask group members to circulate, saying hello to each other, and asking for some piece of information, such as their total weekly income, what they spent most on last year, or something less threatening (and less relevant) such as what they had for breakfast. Tell the group that the person with the money will pass it on to the tenth person that they meet, and that person to the tenth person they meet, etc. If you have a small group, you may need to suggest a number of pieces of information to ask of people, to allow several meetings with the same person.

When you shout stop, find out who has the money, and let them keep it. But ask them to use it to buy biscuits for next week/ flowers for the vicar's wife, or some other suitable expenditure.

sexist

If you have more time, try a scavenger hunt. You could let this happen in the hall you meet in, in your home (if you are very brave), or if you have got thirty to forty minutes and want a bit more fun, in your locality. The usual scavenger hunts consist in finding a selectin of objects, a list of which you can make up from your knowledge of your hall/home/locality.

This is best done as a competitive team event, even if the teams are only pairs, or even if there are only two teams.

If your scavenger hunt is for things, it makes a more natural introduction to the meeting, because a scavenger hunt for things is what most people are involved in most of the time, and an obsession with this is called materialism.

Kick-off

Start by defining materialism (see briefing), outlining its dangers for the Christian, and saying how you will be handling this evening. Sometimes, it's a good idea to explain the structure of a teaching evening before you do it, so that the young people know what's coming. At other times, it's good to keep an element of surprise. Maybe this evening would be an occasion for more openness.

Also, make it clear right at the start that in the Bible there are rich Christians and poor Christians, and that there is nothing wrong with being rich, although it does bring extra responsibilities. The Bible has warnings about Christians trying to get rich, but accepts that some will be rich and others not so well off.

First half

The first half of the teaching will cover what the Bible has to say negatively about the dangers of materialism and the priorities a Christian should have in the use of their possessions. The 'Second Half' will look more positively at how Christians should view their possessions, including their money.

In this part, there are four Bible passages to use, as you will see on the Group Extra sheet. You could cover this as a straight talk, asking people to read out the verses at the appropriate time. Alternatively, focus in on one or two of the passages (try Matthew 6:31–33 and then 1 Timothy 6:6–16). Or divide your group into teams of four, and give each person a copy of the Group Extra sheet and the task of looking at one of the passages, and then reporting back to the group, having answered the question on the Group Extra sheet. Or divide into four groups, each group looking at one passage and then reporting back to the whole. At this point, people can note on their Group Extra sheet what the others said.

Before you start, stress to your group that the Bible has many more references to possessions than these, but these are selected references which summarise much of what the Bible is saying.

You will of course need to have done your homework here, and be prepared to summarise the main points and give guidance where necessary. The 1 Timothy 6 passage may be more difficult than the others, so do give it to the older members if you can.

One other possible method of using this material is to place sheets of paper (A3 or A4) around your meeting room with these headings, one on each:

'Priorities for the Christian'
'Mistakes we make'

Divide up your group as above to look at the four passages and find out what they have to say about these subjects. Then ask group members to write their findings on the relevant sheet around the meeting room.

If you use this method, you will need to draw the strings together, perhaps with a brief summary talk, bringing out the main points from each passage as outlined earlier.

Half-time

Play 'The Expenditure Game'. From the Group Extra sheet, photocopy enough sheets for one for each person. Cut out the money tokens and put one sheet's worth in an envelope and seal it. Do this for each member. Give them the envelopes. Before the meeting, put labels around the room:

'Clothes'
'Books'
'Records'
'Alcohol/cigarettes'
'Sweets and food'
'Holidays'
'Hobbies'
'Transport'
'Give away and entertainment'

By each label put a different coloured felt tip pen. Tell your group members they have £10 to spend (although the tokens in the envelopes add up to more than this to give more flexibility). Ask them to think how they spend their money in an average week, and then to 'spend' their £10 in the same proportion. They spend it by placing it by the appropriate notice, and then shading in the circle on their Group Extra sheet appropriately. At the end of the exercise they should have a pie chart of how they spent their money, coloured in with different colours to represent how their money was spent.

When all have spent (their £10), ask reliable members to add up the total expenditure for each grouping, display this on an OHP or card, and ask members to compare theirs with group results.

Discuss the findings, and ask if there are things Christians should or shouldn't do with their money.

Second half

Focus here on Luke 16:1–15. This looks at the positive side of the Christian use of possessions.

Ask someone to read this out.

Don't be sidetracked by the dishonesty of the way the shrewd manager deals with his master's debtors in verses 5–7. Instead, focus on verse 9, which contains the main point of the parable. This is that God wants us to use all our possessions for his purpose, to further the Gospel. It's not the case that 10% is given back to God and the other 90% is ours to decide what to do with.

All 100% of what we have is ultimately God's, but we have to decide what to do with it. And God wants us to use all we have (possessions, money, the lot) to further the kingdom of God. God gives us worldly wealth to use to bring others to know him, and help them grow in their faith, and therefore to extend the kingdom of God. Trustworthy handling of worldly wealth (v11) means to use it for God's glory. The true riches (v11) are the riches of heaven.

This is not an easy passage to grasp, but this understanding of it makes sense of verses 13–15. There is no change of subject from verse 12 to verse 13. Both are talking about using our money for God, whether it's given away, or spending it on possessions which are then used to bring others to God. This naturally leads on to verse 14, where the Pharisees clearly understood Jesus' meaning, and sneer at him. And the end of verse 14 talks of when money and what it can buy is highly valued by men, it is detestable in God's sight.

As this is not an easy passage, a straight talk from one leader may be advisable. If your group are a little more mature, they may be able to cope with what follows. Break into groups of three or four and give them four possible understandings of the passage.

1 The understanding given above.
2 It's an example for us to follow in dealing with the world.
3 It's a model of faithfulness to our Father in heaven.
4 It's an exhortation to be slightly selfish as we pursue our goal of following Jesus.

Put these up on an OHP or a poster on the wall.

Ask your group to work out which is the correct understanding, and why. Make sure their answers are backed up with careful reference to the passage. After discussion centrally, make sure that everyone is clear about how this addresses positively a Christian's attitude to and use of possessions, both monetary and other.

Final Whistle

In the light of the Luke 16 passage, ask your group to consider how they can use what they own for God. Give each group member a sheet of paper and a pen, and ask them to list five important things that they own.

Then by the side of each of these, ask them to write how they could use it for God. Give suggestions such as lending to friends, teaching me more about Jesus so I can tell my fiends more effectively about him, or making me more mobile so I can give my friends lifts.

Then ask them to write down something they would really like, and then write beside that how they would use it for God. Ask them if their possible use of it for God can justify them buying it, or whether they want it purely for their own use, enjoyment and partial satisfaction.

Extra time

1 Conduct a brief and informal survey of the group's ownership of things like a TV (how many?), VCR, walkman, trainers, CD, microwaves, satellite, etc, and stress that there is in itself nothing wrong with owning any of these, or NOT owning any of them. But our attitude to them (or lack of them) is important.

2 Play Monopoly, or a shortened version of the game.

3 Write a brief case-study of a Christian who is well off but tight-fisted, and wants to be even better off. Ask your group to write a postcard to him or her outlining what the Bible has to say about this.

Equipment

Copies of the Group Extra sheets
Pen and paper
Envelopes for time-tokens
Cut-up time-tokens
Felt-tip pens
OHP/screen or large sheet of paper and pens

Group Extra Sheet

LUKE 12:13–21

What mistakes did the rich farmer make?

What is his basic problem (see v15)?

What did the farmer think life was about?

What *is* life about (vv15, 21)?

MATTHEW 6:31–33

What sort of things should a Christian not worry about (v31)?

What encouragements and promises are here for a Christian?

What are Christian priorities?

What *should* a Christian worry about (v33)?

ECCLESIASTES 5:10–19

What can possessions do and never do?

What shouldn't and should be our attitude to them?

1 TIMOTHY 6:6–16

What dangers does the love of money lead us into?

What should be a Christian's aim in life?

Why do eternal things help us not to love money?
  (vv7,12,13,14)

Circle Pie Chart

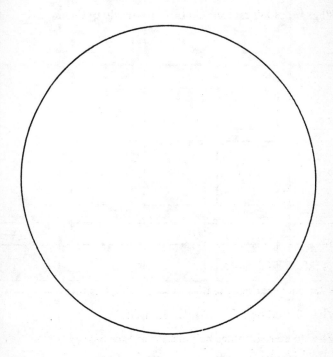

How I Spend My Money

50p	50p	50p	50p	50p
£1	£1	£1	£1	£1
20p	20p	20p	20p	20p
20p	20p	10p	10p	10p
10p	10p	10p	10p	10p
10p	10p	10p	£5	

9

But Don't Stop Here

The aim of this book has been to help you stand on your own two feet as a youth leader, and however experienced you are, to help you take steps forward and be a slightly better leader.

It's all a bit like teaching your child to ride a bike.

You can tell them what to do. You can trot alongside with your hand on the saddle. But sooner or later you have to let go and see how they get on. Training in leadership is a bit like that. There comes a time when you let go, and see what happens.

This book is about to let go.

But before it does, here are a few things to remember.

1 Keep Your Chin Up

Being a youth leader can be a terribly frustrating and depressing business. The difficulties can seem overwhelming. And if you get into that situation, even the good things seem to have a big black cloud hanging over them. So we need to see things in perspective.

People outside the situation are very useful, as they keep things in proportion. Don't get so immersed in your youth group that you lose all outside friends and interests, and become someone with only one topic of conversation.

And think positive. Look back and see how God has worked in the past, and look out for the good points in the present situation.

2 Keep the 'L' Plates

Now that you've read the book, don't think that you know all there is to know about youth work.

We are all learners, and there is always room for improvement and refinement. There will always be areas to work on and new things to learn.

So keep wearing the 'L' plates. Go to training events and read other books about youth work. Talk to other leaders and always be on the lookout to *learn*.

Occasionally, take a candid look at yourself as a youth leader, assess your strengths and weaknesses, and set yourself targets for the next year. Or better still, ask a good friend to help you with this. And make sure you look back at the end of the year to see how you have got on.

Disciples are literally 'learners'. That's as true in youth work as much as in every other area of our Christian lives.

3 Keep up the Discipline

This book has been suggesting some hard work. It's much easier to go back to old ways and not put in the hours. If you are an experienced leader, it's easier to take short cuts which 'no-one will notice'.

To carry on doing what I have been outlining will need discipline. I find it far easier to take the short cuts than to practice what I preach. But in the long run, teaching our groups the Bible properly is the only way that will bear lasting spiritual fruit.

4 Keep Telling Others

We can help each other to keep up the good work by mutual encouragement and exhortation. And you can help others to teach the Bible by talking about the way that you work with your group. Certainly within your leadership team, teach and train each other in this vitally important task. Do you make comments on each other's contributions to the teaching evenings? Do you point out the good parts? Do you talk about possible areas for improvement?

We can help each other to teach the Bible. Let's not do it in isolation.

5 Keep it on the Programme

As you plan your next programme, make sure that it has elements where the Bible is taught. Occasional discussion evenings are fine. So are occasional video evenings. But the staple diet should be sessions in which the Bible is taught. It's this steady, faithful, week by week work which is the basis of real spiritual progress.

As you are planning the next programme, give a thought to the possibility of teaching consecutively through a Bible book. This will help you and your members see the passages in context, and gain an overall grasp of one particular Bible book. There aren't many resources around to help, but a book like James may be a good challenge for a team of leaders to tackle together.

6 Keep Thinking Long Term

Teaching the Bible often has few visible results. Other methods of youth work often seem to be more successful. It is therefore very tempting to go back to the outwardly more successful methods if times get tough.

Have the courage of your convictions.

In depth, powerful, significant work often takes a long time to show on the surface.

The Bible also teaches us to expect some failures. The parable of the sower (Mark 4:1–20, Luke 8:1–15), talks of disappointment when the word is taught, but also the certainty of fruit. Some reject the message. Others accept it but then fall away. But others 'hear it, accept it, and produce a crop' (Mark 4:20).

Wherever the word of God is taught, those are the inevitable reactions. That helps us understand what happens in our groups as we teach them the Bible. It also gives us cause for great confidence as we do this.

And Finally . . .

I hope this book has been informative, instructive and challenging, but not over-awing. Don't get the idea that I'm a super-hero youth leader who does all these things all the time.

I'm not, and I don't.

I'm just an ordinary leader with a small group who works week by week trying to put into practice the sorts of things that I've been talking about. It's not always easy. But it is usually enjoyable. And it's always fulfilling. There is nothing to beat the thrill when your group are studying the word of God and the penny drops, they understand something for the first time, and their eyes are opened.

It's a vast privilege to be part of that. It's humbling to be entrusted with the task of teaching young people the Bible at a time of life when they are at their most receptive, when they are making important decisions, and when many take important spiritual steps forward.

It really is the best job in the world.